CAN COLLEGE LEVEL THE PLAYING FIELD?

CAN COLLEGE LEVEL THE PLAYING FIELD?

Higher Education in an Unequal Society

Sandy Baum and
Michael McPherson

PRINCETON UNIVERSITY PRESS

PRINCETON AND OXFORD

Published by Princeton University Press
41 William Street, Princeton, New Jersey 08540
99 Banbury Road, Oxford OX2 6JX

press.princeton.edu

All Rights Reserved

Library of Congress Cataloging-in-Publication Data

Names: Baum, Sandy (Sandra R.), author. | McPherson, Michael, author.
Title: Can college level the playing field? : higher education in
    an unequal society / Sandy Baum and Michael McPherson.
Description: Princeton : Princeton University Press, 2022. |
    Includes bibliographical references and index.
Identifiers: LCCN 2021035181 (print) | LCCN 2021035182 (ebook) |
    ISBN 9780691171807 (hardback) | ISBN 9780691210933 (ebook)
Subjects: LCSH: College attendance—Social aspects—United States. |
    People with social disabilities—Education (Higher)—United States. |
    Education, Higher—Aims and objectives—United States. | Education,
    Higher—Social aspects—United States. | BISAC: EDUCATION /
    Higher | POLITICAL SCIENCE / Public Policy / Social Policy
Classification: LCC LC148.2 .B38 2022 (print) | LCC LC148.2 (ebook) |
    DDC 378.1/980973—dc23
LC record available at https://lccn.loc.gov/2021035181
LC ebook record available at https://lccn.loc.gov/2021035182

British Library Cataloging-in-Publication Data is available

Editorial: Peter Dougherty, Alena Chekanov
Production Editorial: Terri O'Prey
Text Design: Layla Mac Rory
Jacket/Cover Design: Layla Mac Rory
Production: Erin Suydam
Publicity: Alyssa Sanford, Kathryn Stevens

This book has been composed in Arno, Brothers OT and Industry

10 9 8 7 6 5 4 3 2 1

We dedicate this book to our grandchildren:
Margaret, Frances, Sadie, and Naomi McPherson;
Theodore and James Baum Schwerin Fischer; and those
yet to be born. They bring us joy. We hope that they will
join with others in building a better society than the
one into which they were born.

CONTENTS

ACKNOWLEDGMENTS

Many friends, colleagues, and family members helped us to think through the ideas in this book. We are grateful to all of them. Our editor Peter Dougherty provided strong encouragement and waited patiently while we worked. David Baime, Harry Brighouse, Catherine Bond Hill, and Kailey Mullane read earlier drafts of the book and made very helpful comments and suggestions. Rachel Schwerin's skilled editing significantly improved our writing.

Michael McPherson is deeply grateful to the Spencer Foundation for providing a working and learning environment that supported his early work on this project. The W. T. Grant Foundation provided funding that allowed us to benefit from the excellent work of Urban Institute research assistant Victoria Lee.

For each of us writing this book is the culmination of years of professional experiences, exchanges of ideas, and reading of others' work. Our own personal and professional collaboration is a privilege we cannot imagine doing without.

CAN COLLEGE
LEVEL THE
PLAYING FIELD?

CHAPTER 1
Introduction

The United States is one of the most unequal countries in the developed world and inequality is growing. Reversing this trend is vital to our nation's future. It is not just the gaps in income and wealth that are unacceptable. Individuals have vastly unequal opportunities to end up at the top (or the bottom) of the ladder—no matter how hard they work, how smart they are, or how lucky they are (excepting only luck in their "choice" of parents).

Higher education generates seemingly contradictory realities, acting as both an instrument for improving individuals' economic status and a means of reproducing social inequality over generations. This book analyzes and evaluates the role of higher education in creating and reducing inequality—and in the different but related function of facilitating economic mobility for some while creating barriers for others.

Our goal is to shed light on how the expansion of education, which used to be referred to as "the great leveler," may now exacerbate rather than attenuate inequality. Has something gone fundamentally wrong? Should higher education now be viewed as a cause of, not the cure for, widening income gaps and diminished opportunity?

Our central thesis is that to remedy inequalities in access to higher education opportunities and their outcomes we must both mitigate the inequalities facing children and diminish the extreme variation in labor market rewards facing students as they emerge from school and move on through their working lives. The starting points for the next generation of children are determined by the level of education, earnings, career status, and wealth of their parents. By the time they reach college age, many young people have had their development shaped by inferior K–12 experiences, poor neighborhoods, inadequate housing and health care, and limited opportunities for emotional and intellectual development. The postsecondary education system must do more to compensate for these problems, but it cannot eliminate their effects. Compensating at later ages for the effects of early inequalities in children's treatment and opportunity is more expensive, less effective, and more limited in reach than preventing the inequalities in the first place.

Access to education—and in this day and age particularly to higher education—is supposed to help solve these problems. Although going to college does not pay off for everyone (and there are some colleges that fail most of their students), higher education dramatically increases the chances that people will do well in life, no matter where they started out. Just 8 percent of adults with only a high school education are among the highest-income 20 percent of families in the United States, compared with 38 percent of those with a bachelor's degree or higher; 27 percent of the first group and 7 percent of the second are in the lowest fifth of the income distribution.[1]

1. U.S. Census Bureau, *Current Population Survey Tables for Family Income, 2020,* table FINC-06.

The Problems of Inequality
and Limited Mobility

Which quintile you wind up in matters more now than it did fifty years ago. The share of income held by the families in the top fifth rose from 41 percent in 1967 to 49 percent in 2017; the bottom fifth's share fell from 5.4 percent to 3.8 percent over these years.[2] Inequality in the distribution of wealth is even greater. In 2016 the top 10 percent of earners had 50 percent of household income; the top 10 percent of households held 78 percent of the wealth.[3]

Inequality is a problem because it means that people at the lower end live with so much less than others—not just in material terms but in terms of the opportunities associated with access to resources. Life expectancy is correlated with social status, not only because of unequal access to health care and behavioral differences related to smoking, exercise, and diet. Evidence also suggests that people with less sense of control over their daily lives and less autonomy at work are more susceptible to a range of health problems.[4]

A growing number of economists worry that the resources wealthy individuals and corporations expend on preserving their economic and political advantages may actually reduce the economy's capacity for economic growth.[5] Extreme inequality also threatens our political democracy, both through the overt influence of lobbying and political advertising and through a less visible tendency to equate the interests of the society to the interests of the most wealthy and powerful.

2. Ibid., table FINC-02.
3. Kent and Ricketts, "What Wealth Inequality in America Looks Like."
4. Marmot, *Status Syndrome*.
5. Stiglitz, *The Price of Inequality*.

As the level of income and wealth inequality grows, the consequences of low social mobility grow more severe: the bigger the gaps in income between points on the income distribution—the 20th percentile versus the 40th, for example—the more it matters that it is hard to move up. (As the late economist Alan Krueger put it, the rungs on the ladder of economic status grow further and further apart.)[6]

Moving up the ladder is, however, just one type of mobility—relative mobility is the change in one's position relative to others. By definition, if one person moves to a higher rung, another moves down. Someone will always be at the top and someone else will always be at the bottom. The problems arise not only when the top and the bottom are very far apart but also when individuals' positions are closely tied to where they started out—when the accident of birth matters more than innate capacity and how individuals use their capacities.

There is another form of mobility that is not a zero-sum game. An economy that grows richer over time creates the possibility that all children might be better-off than their parents; everyone can in principle experience absolute mobility, moving up to a higher standard of living than that of their parents. Higher education is fundamental to providing the human capital—the skills and knowledge—that drives the economy forward, enabling society as a whole to become wealthier. If that growth in social wealth is widely shared (as was more the case in the United States from the 1940s to the 1970s than it has been more recently), it becomes feasible for most families to live better than their parents did.[7]

This distinction between absolute and relative mobility helps in sorting through the apparent inconsistencies of higher

6. Krueger, "The Rise and Consequences of Inequality."
7. Chetty et al., "The Fading American Dream."

education's role. There is overwhelming evidence that even though it does not work out for every student who enrolls, college education is a key agent of upward mobility for individuals. College graduates are much more likely than others to end up on a higher rung of the socioeconomic ladder than their parents occupied. Moreover, higher education increases the skills and productivity of the workforce, making it more likely that the economy will grow, and absolute mobility will be widespread—each generation will be better-off than the preceding one.

At the same time, economic inequality is produced and reproduced across generations. Children who start out with a "leg up" because they are born into a higher-income family tend to preserve or extend their advantage as their lives progress. As these children mature into adulthood and parenthood, they pass on their advantages to their own children, a process that continues throughout life. There is a cycle of reproduction of inequality, in which the circumstances of each successive generation condition the circumstances of the next.

Over the last several decades, this cycle of inequality has grown increasingly intense. At every stage of life, forces that make for greater inequality have been gaining strength. The gap in spending on children's education by rich and poor families has continued to grow. The wage gap between those with more and less education grew dramatically in the 1980s and 1990s and has stayed near its historic peak since then. The power of labor unions has faded while CEO salaries have exploded. Taxes have become less progressive and estate taxes have nearly vanished. Countervailing forces are not entirely absent: the Earned Income Tax Credit, the Affordable Care Act, and the rising share of Americans who enroll in college are examples. But efforts to push back against the tide of growing inequality have been limited and sporadic.

In the decades that followed World War II, the rate of economic growth was consistently high, but unlike more recent decades, economic gains were widely shared across social classes. This was a benighted era in terms of racial, gender, and social justice, but the economic mechanisms for distributing income worked differently and better than they do today. Highly progressive income taxes, rapidly expanding educational opportunity, norms constraining CEO salaries and therefore limiting the earnings of those reporting to them, and sustained and widespread prosperity were among the factors contributing to a thirty-year period of declining income inequality and expanding economic opportunity. Although the wages of African American men did experience some convergence with those of white men in this era that has been called "the great compression,"[8] racial and gender discrimination prevented many Americans from accessing these opportunities. But each generation started life in more equal economic circumstances and with broader opportunity than the previous one.

In a process of this kind, where every stage in the process drives the next, it can be misleading to single out any particular social institution or stage in the life cycle as uniquely responsible for inequality. In the current era, where the cycle of inequality has become vicious, universal preschool would retard its growth. So would a meaningful tax on inheritances, or a resurgent labor union movement. Movement toward more equal opportunity in higher education would matter too. But no one of these changes could, on its own, alter the course of society. As scholar Anthony Atkinson has put it, "Inequality is embedded in our social and economic structure, and a significant reduction requires us to examine all aspects of our society."[9]

8. Bayer and Charles, "Divergent Paths."
9. Atkinson, *Inequality*, 3.

Preview: Higher Education's Place in an Extremely Unequal Society

If enough people get a good college education, the forces of supply and demand will likely work to lower income gaps, as they have in the past. Despite common complaints about the earnings premium associated with college degrees not rising rapidly enough, a reduction in inequality between those in the upper and lower reaches of the income distribution requires a narrowing of these earnings differences.

But it is not news that higher education also contributes to perpetuating the class structure across generations, in the United States and around the world. Parents with resources prioritize their children's education to maximize their prospects for success. It is not easy for those without the same money, knowledge, and connections to keep up. Access to some higher education institutions—usually those with the most resources and the best outcomes for their students—is limited to those with the strong academic backgrounds that are closely associated with growing up in affluent, educated families and having strong preschool, elementary, and secondary experiences. The colleges and universities where most of those who grew up in less privileged circumstances are enrolled have lesser resources and more uneven outcomes.

From society's point of view, one central purpose of college education is to prepare students to fulfill important social roles. Selecting the candidates most likely to succeed makes sense. We should not expect colleges simply to ignore differences in applicants' developed capacities in deciding whom to admit; colleges should not all practice open admissions. We should expect colleges to seek out students who show great promise in learning. The significant inequality in opportunity for students of different backgrounds to develop their capacities and to be able to communicate them in the application process is a fundamental obstacle in colleges' efforts to promote more widespread access to successful college experiences.

This is not to say the existing sorting and selecting system for higher education is acceptable in either a moral or practical sense. But the system needs reform, not wholesale replacement.

The dramatic differences in the employment conditions and earnings of adults with different levels and types of knowledge, skills, and credentials compound the variation in educational experiences, generating unacceptably large inequalities in standards of living.

Higher education institutions and financing systems can contribute significantly to narrowing gaps in opportunities. But reversing the spiral of inequality across generations requires much broader social reforms. Higher education will not come close to equalizing outcomes for young people from different backgrounds until satisfactory early life conditions are more nearly universal. And higher education's ability to narrow inequalities of income and wealth will be limited until the labor market and the tax and transfer systems do more to create reasonable circumstances for all children.

Higher Education Affects Inequality; Inequality Affects Higher Education

How has higher education contributed to the growing economic and social inequality in our society, and how might it help reverse the problems? Is the role higher education has played consistent with the idea of higher education as an engine for social mobility?

How are higher education institutions and the higher education system in the United States influenced by the realities of operating in a regime of great and growing inequality?

As detailed in chapter 3, the rising payoff to a college education, as represented by the historically large gap in earnings between those who have earned at least a bachelor's degree and those who have not, explains a significant share of the increasing dispersion of incomes. As the earnings of four-year college graduates have grown relative to the stagnant or declining earnings of adults with lesser levels of educational attainment, the gap between the rich and the poor has grown.

But it is not a one-way street. The reality of large and growing inequality itself has major consequences for how higher education institutions and policies operate. Most centrally, growing inequality of incomes in an economy that strongly rewards knowledge and skill raises the educational stakes for all. People with incomes significantly above the average are more likely to own homes and be more stably employed. They are likely to have some accumulated assets that will allow them to survive a crisis like ill health, a natural disaster, or a pandemic in relatively good personal and financial condition. They are much more likely than lower-income families to be able to retire comfortably, leave some inheritance for their children, and help their children with things like buying a house or paying for college.

As these families' resources continue to rise further above those of the majority, they are increasingly intent on making sure they can pass their advantages on to their children. In a society where economic differences are so vast, and the benefits of economic growth go mainly to people with strong educations and high incomes, competition for place is a powerful force; parents seem to get that. In particular, affluent parents see the advantage in investing in their children's education from an early age. The quality of local schools largely determines families' residential choices and the price they will pay for housing. Parents with money also invest heavily in supplementing the education their children are provided at school.[10]

As fewer and fewer families have the resources to finance their children's higher education without assistance, colleges—whose resources are also limited—engage in fierce competition for these students, leading some institutions to offer more amenities that will appeal to this elite group, adding to operating costs and worsening the spiral of tuition prices.[11]

The sorting of students by socioeconomic background into educational institutions whose relative resource levels tend to correspond to those of their students has generated much of the criticism of higher education as reinforcing inequality.

For example, Suzanne Mettler argues that higher education *promotes* inequality:

> Yet today the U.S. system of higher education is evolving into a caste system with separate and unequal tiers. To be sure, more students from all backgrounds attend college and graduate with valuable degrees. But far too many from low-income and middle-class families depart early with no degrees and crippling levels of student debt. U.S. higher education as a whole is increasingly reinforcing rather than reducing class differences—and federal and state government policies need to change course.[12]

Here is how a writer for the *Chronicle of Higher Education* characterized this view:

---

10. Kaushal, Magnuson, and Waldfogel, "How Is Family Income Related to Investments in Children's Learning?"

11. Hill, "American Higher Education and Income Inequality."

12. Mettler, "How U.S. Higher Education Promotes Inequality."

So, for the individual, yes, higher education offers economic opportunity. But if higher education is a ticket—and increasingly *the* ticket—to economic security in this country, there are real imbalances in whose tickets get punched. . . . "The rich are getting richer because of higher education," says Mr. Mortenson, a senior scholar at the Pell Institute for the Study of Opportunity in Higher Education, "and the poor are getting poorer because of it." . . . Higher education "takes the inequality given to it and magnifies it," says Anthony P. Carnevale, director of the Center on Education and the Workforce at Georgetown University. "It's an inequality machine."[13]

The rich are indeed getting richer in our society, and higher education needs to do more to fight that trend. But identifying higher education as the driving force behind this trend risks deflecting attention from other fundamental contributors and, more seriously, from the solutions required to redress the increasingly visible inequities in the society of which our higher education system is an integral part.

Before College

The striking unfairness of the competition for position becomes most visible as children emerge from their teen years. We see a sorting process play out: a fairly small group of those who complete high school then opt out of the education system altogether. Another small group of high school graduates moves steadily toward an extremely promising future, with the advantages offered by well-resourced, selective colleges and universities. Most of the rest struggle for success in a postsecondary system that yields very uneven results. It propels many students

13. Fischer, "Engine of Inequality."

toward greatly improved opportunities and outcomes—and in doing so enables them to make important contributions to the economy and society—but also leaves too many with little to show for their investments of time, energy, and money.

But if we think of this competition for place in higher education and society as a game that begins as children come out of adolescence, we miss most of the story. We are, as it were, tuning in in the seventh inning, and most of the game has already been played. The inequalities that we see when young people reach the college crossroads have been developing since birth or even before. Understanding the potential for higher education to provide opportunities for upward mobility and to reduce inequality requires understanding the circumstances facing young people in the earlier years of their lives.

Children in this country are born into a wide range of circumstances over which they have no control. Gaps in prenatal health, early childhood education, neighborhoods, housing, health care, family structure, elementary and secondary education, and parental resources accumulate long before the question of whether and where young adults go to college arises.

Understanding the inequalities in pre-college experiences and how they affect opportunities for higher education is a prerequisite for understanding the role of higher education and the potential for its improvement.

The Transition to College (or Not)?

The investments we make in college students generally resemble the investments their families, communities, and the larger society have made in them before college.[14] To oversimplify,

14. Education funding patterns differ significantly by state. A 2018 analysis indicated that in 17 states high-poverty school districts received at least 5 percent less funding per

and as documented in chapter 3, the people who went to the "best" high schools go to the "best" colleges. While there are significant exceptions, by and large the people who enroll at more selective colleges and universities (both public and private) attended better-resourced high schools, had more money spent on their out-of-school development, had better health care, and so on. These resource differences aren't the only things that matter, since people certainly differ in their native capacities and in attitudes and habits they develop as children, including curiosity, academic study habits, and ambition. (These attitudes and habits may themselves be in part the product of the material and social circumstances in which children grow up. It's a lot easier to develop good study habits if you have a quiet place to study and lots of encouragement and support.) The material advantages enjoyed by children from affluent families matter a lot: they have a great deal to do with students' ability to present impressive credentials to admissions offices.

After College

Forces at play in the labor market also undercut higher education's role in reducing inequality and promoting mobility. Even if everyone left college with the same skills and credentials, they would not fare equally well in a labor market characterized by gender and racial discrimination, an outsized role for social connections and financial advantages, and numerous other factors that are far from the ideal of perfect competition.

As adults enter the labor force—whether with no college education, with some college but no degree or certificate, or

---

student than low-poverty districts. Only 11 states addressed the needs of low-income students by providing at least 5 percent more per-student funding to high-poverty than to low-poverty districts (Baker, Farrie, and Sciarra, *Is School Funding Fair?*).

with one of a wide range of credentials that carry a message to potential employers—it is easy to think of market forces as determining who lands where and to assume that preparation and skills are appropriately rewarded. Education is certainly a big factor, but as discussed in more detail in chapter 5, social and economic institutions and forces determine who goes into which occupation and what they are paid. Why are schoolteachers paid so much less relative to other professionals in the United States than in many other countries? Why do corporate CEOs pay themselves so much better and get taxed so much less than their counterparts in the mid-twentieth century? The structure of higher education and differences across colleges don't fully explain why Black bachelor's degree recipients earn less than White graduates with similar degrees, or why long after the economy has recovered, students who graduate into a recession lag behind their peers who entered the labor market a couple of years earlier or later.

Systematic economic and political forces have been at work in recent decades, expanding the gap in market earnings between more and less educated workers. Corporations have gained leverage over workers, especially lower-wage workers, through growing concentration in major industries, aggressive campaigns against unions, and devices like non-compete agreements that reduce workers' bargaining strength. Despite reliance on a progressive income tax and a (too weak) social safety net, the United States falls well short of most other high-income countries in helping its citizens avoid extreme poverty (income less than half of the poverty line) and protecting children.

Thus, the increasingly unequal circumstances in which children grow up and are educated result in large measure from parental inequalities that themselves are influenced by labor market, housing, and health care policies, as well as by the U.S.

tax and transfer system. Whatever we do to ameliorate the inequalities that pervade our nation's system of employment, earnings, savings, retirement, and redistribution will tend to make the next generation's educational path easier. If family incomes and wealth were more equal, pre-college preparation and hence college experiences would be more equal too. And less disparity in college outcomes would help equalize labor market outcomes. We need to develop a "virtuous" circle in which improvements at each life stage foster others.

The pervasiveness of inequality throughout our society does not diminish the importance of the role of higher education in counteracting that inequality. If anything, it makes that role more critical. But it does create daunting challenges. It also requires that evaluation of the strengths and weaknesses of the higher education system be informed by the context of what comes before and what comes after in students' lives.

Exploring the Questions

What does it really mean to say that higher education is increasing rather than reducing inequality? We have to ask, "compared to what?" The share of Americans enrolling in college has grown enormously in the United States since the arrival of the Baby Boomers in the 1960s. If, back in the 1960s, higher education had not responded with massive growth, the relative scarcity of college-educated workers would have made their wages go through the roof, while the wages and job prospects of those denied entrance to colleges would have languished. In fact, a major force helping to keep wage inequality in check in the 1960s and 1970s was the nation's growing investment in college. Even now, as we will argue in this book, further national investment in college, educating more students more successfully, needs to be a key element in any strategy for combating the growth of inequality. In this sense higher education has been and should continue to be an essential source of opportunity, especially for those from disfavored communities. We should not want less of it.

But enrolling more students is not enough. Higher education can and should do more to combat inequality. Institutions must focus more on both reducing stratification of students from different backgrounds into different kinds of institutions and increasing the success rates of those who embark on a college education. In addition to the personal rewards associated with achieving educational goals, an increased supply of well-educated college graduates will reduce earnings inequality. While more people than ever have a shot at college, the kind of college they can get to and especially their odds at succeeding once they get in vary enormously, depending largely on their family backgrounds. In later chapters we will show that the colleges attended by lower-income and first-generation students, as well as by students of color, tend to be starved for resources relative to others. We will report evidence that simply funding these schools better can measurably improve student outcomes. That said, claiming that the higher education system should do more to combat inequality is not the same as claiming that higher education caused it.

But this is not the whole story. The fact that individuals have a greater chance of moving up the ladder if they have a college education than if they do not does not necessarily mean that as more people go to college, it will become easier for people to switch places on the ladder. If everyone earned a bachelor's degree, earning a degree would be just enough to stay in place—not to push someone else down. And of course, not all degrees are created equal. If students from privileged backgrounds earn "better" degrees than others, they will maintain their advantage. This issue of the differences across institutions and credentials is one we will examine in depth in the chapters that follow.

The growing return to a college education between 1980 and 2010 has contributed significantly to rising inequality and the continuing high return to college since then has helped sustain that high level. Although many factors, including bargaining power, minimum wages, and other structural issues, affect inequality in earnings, if more people earned college degrees, the increased supply would tend to put downward pressure on the earnings of this group—and the declining supply of those with lower levels of education should increase their earning power as fewer workers are available to fill the less-skilled jobs with relatively low wages. But if the demand for college-educated workers grows more rapidly than the supply, the wage gap—and inequality—will grow.

Is this the fault of higher education? It is a problem if our system is not providing opportunities to all of the students who could benefit. It is also a problem if the system is so differentiated as to produce some degrees that meet the demand for a skilled labor force—but others that represent much lower levels of relevant knowledge and skills. Higher education institutions can solve only a fraction of this problem. Reducing the inequality in pre-college circumstances and in the rewards of the labor market has to be part of the solution.

Nobody should be written off at age eighteen, and there is much more we can and should do to compensate for the unfairness in opportunity that confronts people as they emerge (or don't emerge) from high school, but there is no way we can "fix" higher education in a fundamental way while turning a blind eye to the inequality in condition and in opportunity that faces people from their earliest days. Neither should we overlook the ways in which our economic system magnifies the economic consequences of the educational inequalities with which students emerge from higher education.

Lowering the return to college, both by expanding college success and by implementing policies such as increased minimum wages or guaranteed incomes that raise after-tax income for the less well-off or more progressive tax systems that lower the after-tax incomes of the very well-off, would make education more of a real choice and might limit the over-weighting of earnings growth as the main aim of college.

Moving Forward

We do not pretend to have a magic formula for solving the problems we explore in this book. In fact, we argue that policy proposals that sound like magic bullets are likely to have disappointing results and even exacerbate some of the problems they are designed to solve.

We will argue, to cite a simple but controversial example, that a policy of free public college tuition for all students will do more to strengthen the ability of students from affluent families to secure their status than it will to bolster the opportunities of those who most need help. Similarly, it is not enough to urge states to appropriate more money for public higher education; we also need to ask where the states will direct the funding and how it will be used. We will argue that elite private universities should work to enroll more low-income students, but we are not going to achieve large-scale improvement in student success by massively moving students from less selective to more selective institutions. Instead, we are going to need to focus resources and attention on improving the performance of the institutions students actually attend. Elite institutions can contribute to this effort.

But no efforts focused entirely on higher education can solve the problems of unequal educational opportunities. Instead, we must emphasize investing more in the overall environments and the pre-college education of students from disadvantaged families. And we must address the structural weaknesses of our economy that shape the lives of adults who do not have the benefit of college credentials.

Overview of the Book

The book is organized as follows. Chapters 2 and 3 provide the basic conceptual and empirical foundations for the later chapters. Chapter 2 examines the concepts of inequality, equal opportunity, social mobility, and racial justice at work in discussions of higher education's social role and reports on the current state of empirical evidence on these matters in the United States.

Chapter 3 presents a wealth of data describing the stratification and outcomes gaps that show how variations in college experience fit into the story of how inequality is produced and reproduced in our society

The next two chapters put higher education in the context of unequal lives before college and constrained opportunities in later life. Chapter 4 focuses on how differences in family structures, parenting, neighborhoods, and elementary/secondary education all affect the academic preparation of young people, in addition to their expectations, aspirations, attitudes, and behavior patterns. In chapter 5, we shift our perspective forward to the adults' work lives. Not surprisingly in our knowledge- and technology-driven economy, earnings are closely tied to

educational background. But important as education is in explaining wage gaps, it does not come close to eliminating differences by race and gender. We conclude the chapter by examining the nation's relatively ineffective efforts to redress these
imbalances through a progressive tax-transfer system and our
willingness to tolerate a substantially higher level of extreme
poverty for families with children compared to other high-
income nations. Support for children in the recent pandemic
recovery package provides some hope that the nation will turn
its attention to addressing this vital issue.

Chapter 6 focuses on higher education itself, asking how colleges and universities can best promote more fairness and opportunity and also attenuate those features of higher education
that promote the preservation of privilege. We look first at the
small number of selective, relatively well-resourced institutions
that generally enroll disproportionately affluent student bodies
but argue the work with the greatest impact will be at the broad-
access institutions that educate, and will continue to educate,
the vast majority of students seeking economic security and
upward mobility. There is growing evidence that some programs and practices can significantly increase student success
at non-selective institutions educating students who do not arrive with stellar academic credentials.

In chapter 7 we consider potential public policies that
might strengthen the success of higher education in breaking
down barriers to increasing opportunities for students from
low- and moderate-income backgrounds and in weakening
the link between the circumstances of birth and the life outcomes shaped by educational attainment. We ask how effective these policies can be absent parallel efforts to diminish
pre-college inequities and labor market forces exacerbating
earnings differentials. If our social structures provided more

equal support and opportunities to all children, whether and where young people pursue college education would be much less correlated with family backgrounds.

The idea that there should be differential investment in people with different aptitudes and inclinations toward schooling is reasonable and reflects the fact that a central purpose of college education is to prepare people to fill a wide range of valuable social roles. In addition to the magnitude of the differences in investment in students, the trouble is that the aptitudes and inclinations are not developed under fair conditions. The problem of fair conditions needs to be the long-run focus. The goal of this book is to broaden the focus from the narrow question of the sorting of students into colleges toward the much more fundamental question of how we can create more meaningful options for all members of our society.

Conclusion

In this book, our main focus is on higher education. But our goal is to examine higher education in the context of the larger process of the production and reproduction of inequality—not as an isolated force whose contribution to inequality is independent of what comes before and after in people's lives. We do not focus on higher education because we think it is somehow more central or determinative of economic inequality than other institutions are, and certainly not because we think higher education is easier to change than, say, the tax system or pre-school education. Rather, our focus is here because this is the part of the social system we have studied and about which we think we have something useful to say. Our intention is to modify the common misconception of higher education as itself the cause of either increased inequality or more or less prevalent opportunities for social mobility. The impact and effectiveness of higher education are conditioned on the institutions, the social forces, and the inequalities that shape individuals' early lives and their social and economic circumstances as they mature and nurture the next generation.

The "Great Sorting" that takes place in the United States as students emerge from high school makes *visible* the large inequalities that have been quietly growing in neighborhoods, schools, summer camps, and trips abroad for eighteen years. If and where young people attend college is heavily influenced by their earlier educational and life experiences. Ideally, college could provide the mechanism for erasing the wide range of effects of these early experiences. No matter where or how you grew up, if you can manage to get to college, you should be on a level playing field as you enter your adult life. While this vision may not be realistic, colleges and the governments that support them can and should do much more than we do now. Higher education can't do it all. To get closer to that ideal vision of college, we will need a patient and coordinated effort across all our major social institutions.

CHAPTER 2

Understanding the Issues: Inequality and Mobility

Before we can examine higher education's relationship to inequality and social mobility, we need to understand these concepts. This is not as simple as it sounds, because they are quite different, and each has a number of different meanings.

We begin with inequality.

Inequality

There are many differences among people, and no one expects higher education to have much to do with most of them. But one linkage that does stand out is that between income and education. The longer individuals go to school the higher their incomes tend to be. And the higher a family's income is, the longer their children tend to stay in school. More years of education are also associated with better health and a greater likelihood of voting. Considerable evidence points to education as causing improvements in these economic and non-economic outcomes. In other words, it's not just that people who are likely to be successful workers and active citizens are more likely than others to go to college but that going to college has a positive impact on how individuals' lives turn out.[1] In other words, the relationships are not only correlational but also in part causal. The evidence suggests that moving toward more equal education is likely to reduce inequality in health, in political participation including voting, and in income. Moreover, making incomes more equal has a good chance of creating more equal education for the next generation—and thereby helping to make health and voting propensities more equal, in addition to diminishing other differences in the life experiences of people growing up in varying circumstances.

Most discussion of the role of higher education focuses on the income piece—on economic inequality. "Income" is a useful and familiar, although incomplete and imperfect, index of people's well-being. Along with wealth, it tracks both how much people can consume and how well they are protected against risks. In the absence of a strong social safety net, many low-income households struggle to meet their basic needs. The coronavirus pandemic made these persistent differences all the starker, with members of low-income households being disproportionately the ones who either lost their jobs or had to risk their health and even their lives to work in face-to-face environments—and being least equipped to manage through any loss of income.

Income is also associated with a wide range of nonmonetary differences in people's lives. Those with higher incomes tend to have more autonomy both at work and in the rest of their lives; they have more choice about the neighborhoods they live in

1. Oreopoulos and Petronijevic, "Making College Worth It."

and the way they spend their time. Income also matters for people's social standing: low-income people are often dependent on others while high-income people are often in a position of power relative to others.

Defining and measuring income is not simple. We might focus on individuals or households, on income before or after taking account of taxes and transfers. Income encompasses both what people earn from their labor and the returns the assets they own (their wealth) generate. (Most Americans' assets take the form of the equity they hold in their homes and whatever financial assets they have accumulated in their 401K or other pension vehicles.) The ownership of financial assets outside of pension funds is very concentrated among high-income households.) Cognizant of these complexities, when we report particular numbers or present data, we will be explicit about the measures we are using.[2]

There is much more to well-being than financial resources. Two people can have similar incomes but very different levels of well-being if one of them labors twelve hours a day at a physically demanding or dangerous job while the other lives off the return on inherited assets. Different education levels provide access to different types of occupations, different working conditions, and different social environments. And, as noted, people care about their health and the rewards and satisfactions of their private and public lives.

The Gini coefficient is one of a number of quantitative measures that strive to capture the inequality in the entire distribution of income in one number. It ranges from 0 (complete equality) to 1 (when one person has all the income). More

2. For a detailed treatment of the complexities of income measurement, see Atkinson, *Inequality*, chap. 2.

intuitive measures, like the share of all income received by the top 10 percent or 1 percent of households, the size of the gap between the median income and income at the 90th percentile of the distribution, or the share of households whose incomes are less than half the median income, call attention to different features of the distribution.

Few people believe that everyone should have exactly the same income or wealth, but many are concerned about the wide and growing gaps among individuals and across demographic groups. Much attention goes to families in the top few percent of the income distribution, most of whose members have a bachelor's degree or higher. The share of income going to the highest-income fifth of families rose from 41 percent in 1979 to 47 percent in 1999 and 50 percent in 2019. The share of income accruing to the top 5 percent of families increased by almost half over forty years, from 15 percent to 22 percent. The share going to the lowest-income 20 percent of families fell from 5.4 percent to 4.3 percent to 3.9 percent over these years.[3] This growing inequality is also reflected in other measures like the Gini coefficient, which grew from .404 in 1979 to .458 in 1999 and .484 in 2019.[4]

While the distribution of income across the entire range of individuals or households matters, inequality across groups matters too. In 2019 median income for 35- to 44-year-olds ranged from $42,400 for Hispanic full-time year-round workers and $48,200 for Blacks to $60,900 for Whites and $82,300 for Asians with the same work pattern.[5] Obviously, these income

3. U.S. Census Bureau, *Historical Income Tables, 2020*, table F-2.

4. Ibid., table A-4.

5. U.S. Census Bureau, *Selected Characteristics of People 15 Years Old and Over by Total Money Income in 2019*, PINC-01.

levels are unequal. How unfair this inequality is depends in part on how the differences come about.

Most people approve of some differences in income associated with levels of educational attainment and related job requirements. One reason people invest in education is to increase their earnings opportunities. But differences in educational attainment across racial and ethnic groups are at least partially the result of historical and present-day social and economic discrimination. Moreover, there are considerable differences in earnings between members of different racial and ethnic groups with the same level of education. For example, median earnings of Black 35- to 44-year-old bachelor's degree recipients are about $14,000 less than the median for White adults of the same age with the same level of education. Just 23 percent of full-time Black workers whose highest degree was a bachelor's degree earned more than $100,000 in 2019, compared with 36 percent of Whites.[6]

It is clearly easier to measure inequality than to decide which inequalities are morally problematic. These examples are a good reminder that pointing out that there are inequalities in one or another measure is only the beginning of a conversation about when and why they matter.

Economic inequality is most frequently measured in terms of income disparities. But wealth is even more unequally distributed than income in the United States and this inequality has risen dramatically in recent decades. In 1963, families near the top had six times the wealth of families in the middle. By 2016, they had twelve times the wealth of families in the middle. Between 1963 and 2016, families near the bottom of the wealth

---

6. U.S. Census Bureau, *Educational Attainment: People 25 Years Old and Over, 2019,* PINC-03.

distribution (at the 10th percentile) went from having no wealth on average to being about $1,000 in debt. Those in the middle more than doubled their wealth, while families near the top (at the 90th percentile) saw their wealth increase fivefold. The wealth of those at the 99th percentile grew sevenfold.[7] The share of wealth held by the top 1 percent rose from 25–30 percent in the 1980s to 40 percent in 2016.[8]

In 2016, the median White family in the United States had 4.8 times the median wealth of Hispanic families ($919,000 versus $192,000) and 6.6 times the median wealth of Black families ($140,000). Median Black family wealth doubled (after adjusting for inflation) between 1983 and 2016; median wealth for White and Hispanic families tripled.[9] Whatever other progress our society might have made, the racial wealth gap is only getting larger.

The focus on the very thin slice at the top of the distribution that is exceptionally wealthy—the top 1 percent or top 0.1 percent or the even smaller group of multibillionaires—has increased in recent years, as their share of total income and wealth has grown. While the top 1 percent includes many highly paid professionals who generally hold advanced degrees—doctors and CEOs, for example—the incomes of multibillionaires are more heavily dependent on exceptional skill, luck, and timing as entrepreneurs, or on inherited wealth, than on educational attainment. While the very top incomes garner disproportionate attention, lesser inequalities, like those between the top 20 percent of households and the median household, have been growing too and are probably at least as important in how families view their own circumstances.

7. Urban Institute, "Nine Charts about Wealth Inequality."
8. Zucman, "Global Wealth Inequality."
9. Urban Institute, "Nine Charts about Wealth Inequality."

One of the questions we want to address in this book is whether and how higher education has played a role in increasing income and wealth inequality—and what kinds of policies and practices might help reduce that inequality in the future. We also want to know how increasing inequality has affected colleges and universities and their students, including the role higher education plays in enabling families to pass on their advantages to the next generation.

Poverty

A problem closely related to inequality is poverty—both relative and absolute. Poverty is one core factor that makes the high level of inequality prevailing in the United States today a problem even for those who don't think inequality is bad in itself: there is a floor below which someone's income or standard of living is simply too low. It's not so much that some people have too much in an absolute sense—although the eye-popping fortunes that have emerged in recent years certainly raise that question—as that others simply do not have enough to manage in any reasonable way. How much households at the lower end of the distribution struggle depends on the dollar values of their incomes and the circumstances of their lives, including their health and family size. The needs to be met go beyond the simply physical requirements for nutrition and shelter. In a democratic society, a minimum level of income is needed for dignity and social recognition. For those who are responsible for children, it is also essential that those children have both their physical and developmental needs met—a consideration that connects directly to the notion of equal opportunity, which we discuss below.

If people don't have enough resources to buy food, pay for housing, and attend to their children's needs, they are living in absolute poverty. But beyond that, levels of well-being also depend on relative status. People need to live in conditions compatible with their dignity and sense of self-worth by the standards of their society.[10] An obvious illustration is that some households living below the poverty line in the United States might not seem poor in Somalia. But that does not make their deprivations in the United States any less acute.

Reducing absolute poverty is a straightforward task in principle. We could simply provide more resources to the households whose incomes fall below some specified cutoff, such as the official poverty line, ensuring that no one lives below that level. Welfare state or "safety net" policies play this role, and many countries come closer to meeting that aim than the United States has managed to do. But there could still be relative poverty if some households have much less than others. Relative poverty might be defined as having an income below say half of the overall median, based on the judgment that this is the minimum adequate level of living to establish people as full members of society. This measure would be connected to inequality from the standpoint of what a "normal" living standard is in the society, but not much connected to how much money the richest people make.

The education people receive clearly has a connection to their likelihood of living in poverty. A very small share of households that include an individual with a college degree are in poverty. In 2019, when 19 percent of adults ages 25 and older lived below the poverty line, poverty rates were 24 percent for those without a high school diploma, 12 percent for high school graduates with no college education, 8 percent for those with some college but no degree, and 4 percent for those with a

10. See King, "The American Dream"; Marmot, *Status Syndrome*.

bachelor's degree or higher.[11] It is reasonable to believe that if fewer people had very low levels of educational attainment, fewer would live below the poverty line. But there would still be a question of how many people would be in relative poverty, defined in terms of distance from the median.

Why Does Inequality Matter?

While the case for addressing absolute poverty is persuasive to most people, concerns about inequality are less straightforward. If everyone had a reasonable standard of living, should we object to people having extremely high incomes? Perhaps not, but Robert Frank has made a strong case that most of the resources of the very wealthy are spent on positional goods— simply trying to consume more lavishly than their fellow gazillionaires. If the wealthy all kept their relative positions but simply shrank the size of their estates, they would suffer little or no loss in welfare. Frank presents substantial evidence that a significant share of society's resources are going into goods and services that don't actually increase anyone's well-being.[12] Whether or not this is unfair, it is not efficient.

Other reasons for limiting inequality relate to its consequences. If income and wealth are highly concentrated among a small fraction of the population it will be very difficult for those not born into this privileged class to improve their lot in life— mobility will be seriously constrained. The distances between rungs on the ladder will widen and the well-off will work harder to ensure that they pass opportunities on to their children. Those not winning the birth lottery will be deprived not only of resources but of opportunity.

11. U.S. Census Bureau, *Income and Poverty in the United States, 2019*, table B-1.
12. Frank, "Positional Externalities."

Moreover, there is a strong connection between money and political power in democratic societies.[13] People with extreme wealth have disproportionate power to make their views heard and to shape the electoral chances of candidates for office. This is an exceptionally strong consideration in the United States because of Supreme Court rulings that regard spending money on campaigns as a protected form of free expression. Apart from the extremely wealthy, the merely affluent also have disproportionate voice because they have the time and the money to promote their views and because we live in an advertising-driven media culture that pushes attention toward the perspectives and concerns of the more affluent.[14] The growing concentration of economic power in a handful of firms, most noticeably in computer technology and internet-based communications, leads to great wealth and enormous political voice among a handful of extraordinarily powerful men (and a few women).

Traditionally, economists have tended to argue that there is a trade-off between increasing equality and increasing economic growth. Arthur Okun, a member of President Kennedy's Council of Economic Advisers, introduced the idea of the "leaky bucket."[15] The idea was that transferring money from the rich to the poor is like carrying water in a leaky bucket—some of it is lost along the way so there is a trade-off between the increase in equality and maximizing efficiency—the whole pie gets smaller.

But, as Okun agreed, public policies such as those that foster education can increase both equality and efficiency. The concept of "human capital," popularized in the mid-1960s by free-market economist Gary Becker, connects differences in earnings with

13. Bartels et al., "Inequality and American Governance."
14. Jacobs and Skocpol, *Inequality and American Democracy.*
15. Okun, *Equality and Efficiency.*

differences in individuals' capabilities, skills, and knowledge—
their human capital.[16] A clear implication of this now standard
fundamental economic concept is that increasing human capital
through education will increase both society's productivity and
the earnings of the newly educated. In other words, we can have
growth *and* increasing opportunity for the least well-off.

Nobel Laureate Joseph Stiglitz and others have argued that
beyond some point increases in inequality become counterproductive for economic growth. These economists argue that ex-
cessive inequality tends to produce macroeconomic instability
and to absorb resources in defending existing market power
rather than investing in innovation.[17]

Americans seem to be more accepting of inequality than
people in other countries at least partially because they believe
that it is possible to get ahead if they work hard. In other words,
inequality doesn't seem so bad—even to those in the lower part
of the income distribution—if there is a lot of economic mobility, with meaningful opportunities for all individuals regardless
of their starting points.[18]

Mobility

A central component of the American Dream is the idea that
people who start out with minimal resources have the opportunity to move up the ladder. Social mobility involves people
moving up (and down) the strata of a social system. Such movement is impossible in a caste or a feudal society, where one's
social status is formally decided at birth. By definition mobility

16. Becker, *Human Capital*.
17. Stiglitz, *The Price of Inequality*.
18. Isaacs and Sawhill, "Reaching for the Prize."

is only possible when some of the characteristics determining social status are shaped by one's own actions and choices.

Relative Mobility

Many Americans hold the optimistic belief that the United States is a highly mobile society in which one's economic status is determined mainly by one's own talents and motivation and is not much influenced by status at birth. This view is not well supported by facts. Children are more likely to remain at the relative position of their parents in the United States than in most other developed countries. A larger share of earnings differences is passed from one generation to the next in the United States and the United Kingdom than in other developed Western countries.[19] Moving up from the bottom is particularly difficult in the United States.[20]

The ideal of equal opportunity is not fully captured by the notion of high levels of social mobility. A society in which most people routinely played the lottery for high stakes would have a lot of economic mobility, but it would mainly be determined by random events. The ideal of a society with equal opportunity is that the major features of your life depend on your own efforts, ambitions, and talents, not simply on your parents' income or social status, or on dumb luck. The equal opportunity ideal also extends beyond economic mobility, because it concerns not just making a lot of money but having the kind of work and life you desire and are willing to work for. The American Dream is not only "anybody can grow up to be rich" but also "anybody can grow up to be president."

19. Corak, "Do Poor Children Become Poor Adults?"
20. Jäntti et al., "American Exceptionalism in a New Light."

Social status is not always the same as economic status. Some professions require considerable skills and may garner respect without paying high wages. Individuals who have completed prestigious postsecondary degrees may have high social status even if they are not wealthy. Buying the right lottery ticket can immediately propel winners to the top of the economic scale without necessarily changing their occupation or social status.

That said, much of the economic immobility observed in the United States is the result of inequalities in educational opportunity, childhood health status, and general developmental environments that are very difficult to reconcile with any plausible understanding of equal opportunity. Thus, data on social mobility provide much useful information, even if they do not tell the whole story.

Acquiring more education clearly enhances the probability of moving upward. As detailed in chapter 3, among adults without a bachelor's degree whose parents were in the lowest-income fifth of the population, almost half remain in this income group in adulthood. Among those from similar backgrounds who have earned bachelor's degrees, more than 80 percent are in higher-income groups as adults.[21] In other words, education clearly generates mobility for individuals who manage to progress through the system.

However, children growing up in families that are already high on the totem pole have the greatest opportunities to access high-quality education—from early childhood on. This unequal educational opportunity contributes to the stability of an unequal income distribution. Only 4 percent of children born to parents with income in the lowest quintile end up in the highest quintile while 43 percent remain in the bottom quintile; meanwhile,

21. Haskins, "Education and Economic Mobility."

40 percent of children born to parents in the highest quintile stay there, with only 8 percent falling to the bottom quintile.[22]

Relative mobility is even lower for Black children than for White children. Black children who are born in the bottom quartile based on a long-term measure of income are nearly twice as likely to remain there as adults as are White children whose parents had identical incomes and are four times less likely to reach the top quartile. The difference in mobility for Blacks and Whites persists even after controlling for a host of parental background factors, children's education and health, and whether the household was female-headed or receiving public assistance.[23] We suspect that differences in family wealth, reflecting the legacy of slavery and housing discrimination, help to explain this finding, but data linking such wealth differences to mobility are hard to come by.

Higher education fosters upward mobility for those who succeed in earning high-quality degrees. But the barriers to accomplishing this are far greater for those who grow up in families with very limited resources—and for Black people—than for those from more privileged backgrounds.

The Relationship between Inequality and Social Mobility

Growth in inequality of income for one generation leads to greater inequality of opportunity for the next. The larger the gaps among people, the more difference relative position makes in standard of living and other aspects of people's lives.

---

22. Greenstone et al., "Thirteen Economic Facts about Social Mobility and the Role of Education."

23. Hertz, *Understanding Mobility in America*, 4.

The late economist Alan Krueger described the relationship between these two phenomena in a graph that has come to be known as the Great Gatsby Curve. Parents' financial circumstances predict the circumstances of their adult children most strongly in countries with high levels of income inequality. Krueger's image of inequality as representing rungs on a ladder, noted in chapter 1, is helpful here. The farther apart those rungs are, the more difficult it is to ascend them.

For example, Denmark, Norway, Finland, and Sweden have low inequality and high social mobility from generation to generation. The United States, the United Kingdom, and Italy do relatively poorly on both measures (figure 2.1). In Finland, Norway, and Denmark less than one-fifth of any economic advantage or disadvantage that a father may have had is passed on to a son in adulthood. In Italy, the United Kingdom, and the United States, roughly 50 percent of any advantage or disadvantage is passed on.[24]

The work of Raj Chetty and his colleagues that focuses particularly on the share of college students who move from the lowest quintile of the income distribution to the highest has shone a bright light on the role of higher education institutions in promoting this type of economic mobility.[25] But relative mobility is a zero-sum game. Since at any given time only 20 percent of persons can be in the top 20 percent, if one person moves up to a higher rank, another must move down. Another way to measure economic mobility is to ask whether people have a higher standard of living than their parents. Economic growth makes it possible for everyone to be better-off than the previous generation.

24. Krugman, "The Great Gatsby Curve"; Corak, "Income Inequality."
25. Chetty et al., "Is the United States Still a Land of Opportunity?"

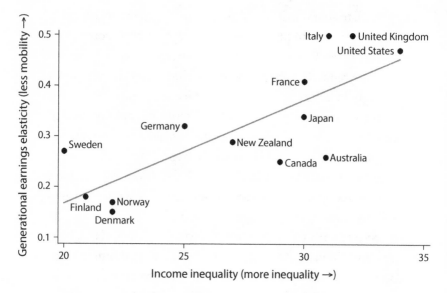

FIGURE 2.1. The Great Gatsby Curve
Countries with higher levels of income inequality tend to have less economic mobility across generations.

Note: Income inequality is measured as the Gini coefficient, using disposable household income for about 1985 as provided by the OECD. Intergenerational economic mobility is measured as the elasticity between paternal earnings and a son's adult earnings, using data on a cohort of children born, roughly speaking, during the early to mid-1960s and measuring their adult outcomes in the mid- to late 1990s. The estimates of the intergenerational earnings elasticity are derived from published studies, adjusted for methodological comparability.
Source: Corak, "Income Inequality," figure 1.

Absolute Mobility

Raj Chetty and his colleagues have documented the decline over time in absolute mobility in the United States. According to the Opportunity Insights website the percentage of children earning more than their parents declined from 90 percent for those born in 1945 to 70 percent for those born in 1955, 59 percent for those born in 1965, 57 percent for those born in

1975, and 50 percent for those born in 1985. Chetty and his colleagues attribute part of this decline to slower overall growth but argue that it is caused primarily by the distribution of the benefits of that growth, which have gone almost exclusively to people with higher incomes.[26]

This point is worth dwelling on. By some measures, relative social mobility in the United States has not gotten worse over time. But the great majority of the Baby Boom generation grew up to live at a higher standard than their parents. Discrimination prevented some groups—notably Black Americans—from reaping their share of the benefits. But as the economy grew, most people shared in the wealth—in fact the income gains were higher in percentage terms for those with lower incomes than for others. For many Americans this was a reasonable approximation of the American Dream. The terms on which gains were shared might not be fair, but most people did share in the gains. Even though it may have been as hard then as it is now to get to the top, a greater fraction of Millennials than of Baby Boomers face the risk that they will wind up with a lower standard of living than their parents had.

26. Chetty and colleagues are not the only scholars to study absolute mobility across generations, although they have by far the largest data set because of their unique access to IRS data. Studies using different data sets, different estimation dates, and different ages at which the comparison is made yield somewhat different quantitative findings. There is little disagreement that the extent of absolute mobility has fallen over time, but researchers have shown that different decisions about measurement (such as the choice of age at which the comparison is made, the deflator used to adjust for changes in living standards over time, and others) might raise the estimate of the fraction of children reaching a higher income than their parents as high as two-thirds or more. Winship (*Economic Mobility in America*) provides a thorough literature review.

Conclusion

In this chapter we have introduced the central ideas of income
and wealth inequality, economic mobility, both relative and absolute, and equal opportunity. We provided selected data on
where the United States stands on these metrics. For those who
value equality and mobility, the news is not good. And for a
country built on the myth and the only partly realized ambition
of continual progress, the realities described carry profound
political and social implications.

For several decades following World War II, the U.S. economy expanded rapidly, with only relatively few and relatively
mild recessions, and increasing incomes were widely shared
across the income distribution. The rising tide was, indeed, raising many boats. All this happened even as the nation became
the world's most powerful economy and the undisputed leader
of the free world. Over the 1950s, 1960s, and 1970s many Americans came to believe that theirs was a land of widespread educational and economic opportunity, growing prosperity, and
high social mobility. And with very important qualifications,
especially regarding marginalized racial groups and women,
there was an important element of truth in their belief.

But this era of widely shared prosperity came rather abruptly
to an end in the late 1970s, and since then we have lived through
forty years of low mobility, fading educational and economic opportunity, and significantly slowed economic growth. It has taken
a long time for this truth to sink in with the public, who have
clung to the view that, even if equality in incomes is not what it
once was, America still enjoys widespread mobility and a good
chance for anyone to succeed. Unfortunately, this really isn't so.

It is important to dispense with illusions about American
exceptionalism regarding equality, opportunity, and mobility.

And in this chapter, we have described the discouraging realities about the nation's present condition. But this necessary disillusionment should not lead either to despair or to a search for some kind of magic bullet that will abruptly reverse our course of growing inequality. The forces of society have great momentum. We arrived in the current unequal circumstances over a long and checkered history, with severe limitations on the options available to Black people, women, and other groups. First slowing and then reversing the trend toward greater inequality and reduced opportunity will be the work of generations and it will involve all our major social and economic institutions, not least education, including higher education.

We turn next to the task of describing how higher education operates in our increasingly unequal society.

CHAPTER 3

Inequality in Higher Education: Who Goes to College? Where Do They Enroll? Which Credentials Do They Earn?

The idea that college can mitigate inequality or promote socio-economic mobility is rooted in the reality that higher levels of education correspond to higher incomes. Children from low-income backgrounds are much more likely to rise above the economic status of their parents if they complete college degrees than if they end their education after high school. However, college outcomes are a central factor leading children from high-income families to preserve their advantage. In a society where opportunities to prepare for a demanding college education are so unevenly distributed, gaps in participation and success in higher education help to explain this apparent contradiction.

In addition to being important factors influencing economic opportunities and outcomes, educational opportunities and outcomes are critical in their own right. For many people education is intrinsically a valuable experience and plays an important role in opening the doors to opportunities and experiences in life that are not entirely—and sometimes not at all— economic. For example, the opportunity for people with talent and passion for music to develop their capacities or for those with great scholarly potential to realize it through education is of fundamental importance, size of one's paycheck aside. Higher levels of education are also associated with better health, more active civic participation, greater capacity to support children's development, and a range of other differences in attitudes, behaviors, and opportunities. In other words, data on college participation and outcomes—the focus of this chapter—are critical both for understanding the relationship between higher education and economic inequality and for gaining a broader understanding of how the wide-ranging personal benefits of higher education are distributed across the population.

Black and Hispanic youth, those from low-income backgrounds, and those whose parents are not college educated are less likely than others to complete high school. If they complete high school, they are less likely to go to college. If they do go to college, they are less likely to go to public or private nonprofit four-year institutions. If they go to these institutions, they are less likely to attend selective institutions.

All of these circumstances—reflecting in significant measure the childhood experiences documented later in chapter 4— contribute to unequal outcomes. Those from less-privileged backgrounds are less likely to complete their programs and if they do complete them, they are more likely than others to earn short-term certificates or associate degrees, as opposed to the bachelor's degrees that are more common among White and Asian students, those from higher-income families, and those whose parents earned at least a bachelor's degree.

Understanding the nature of the inequalities in college participation and outcomes provides insight into how changes in public policy relating to the structure and financing of postsecondary education, as well as potential actions on the part of higher education institutions, might mitigate these inequalities.

Higher Levels of Education Correspond to Higher Incomes

In 2019, median earnings for 35- to 44-year-olds whose highest degree was a bachelor's degree were $62,000—68 percent higher than the $37,000 median for high school graduates. Those in this age group who had completed advanced degrees earned 2.2 times as much as high school graduates. Even those with some college but no degree earned 14 percent ($5,000) more per year than the median for those who had no college education (figure 3.1).

The higher median earnings associated with higher levels of education do not, of course, mean that everyone with a bachelor's degree earns more than anyone without a college education. Figure 3.1, which displays the 25th and 75th percentiles of earnings for each group in addition to the median, shows the overlap. In 2019, 19 percent of high school graduates earned more than the median of $62,000 for BA recipients and 21 percent of four-year college graduates earned less than the median of $37,000 for high school graduates. But these exceptions do not change the reality of the earnings premium accruing to most people who complete college degrees.

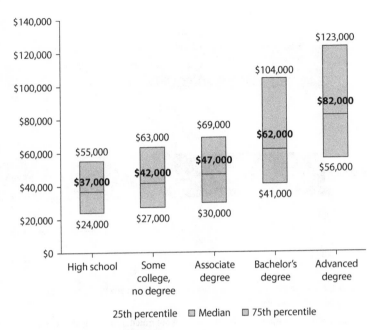

FIGURE 3.1. Median Earnings of 35- to 44-Year-Olds by Educational Attainment, 2019
Median earnings rise with level of education.

Note: Includes all individuals ages 35 to 44 with earnings; 75th percentile is estimated for bachelor's and advanced degrees because published data are top-coded.
Source: U.S. Census Bureau, *Current Population Survey*, Annual Social and Economic Supplement, 2020, table PINC-03.

College Degrees Are Central to Economic Mobility

A Brookings Institution study compared the incomes of adult children who were about age 40 between 1995 and 2002 to their parents' incomes at the same age. Among those who had earned bachelor's degrees, 74 percent had higher (inflation-adjusted)

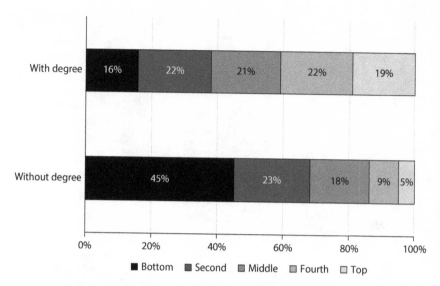

FIGURE 3.2. Income Quintile of 40-Year-Olds (1995 to 2002) Whose Parents Were in the Lowest Income Quintile
Children who grow up in low-income families are much more likely to move up the income ladder if they earn a four-year degree.

Source: Haskins, "Education and Economic Mobility."

earnings than their parents had at the same age. Among those without a bachelor's degree, just 63 percent surpassed their parents. Among those whose parents had been in the lowest income quintile, 96 percent of those with a bachelor's degree and 81 percent of those without this degree earned more than their parents had (figure 3.2).

Another way of seeing the association between earning a college degree and moving up in the income distribution is to look at where those who started at the bottom ended up. As figure 3.2 indicates, 16 percent of those who earned a bachelor's degree remained in the lowest income quintile as adults, compared with 45 percent of those who did not graduate from a four-year college. Nineteen percent of college graduates and 5 percent of non-graduates whose parents were in the lowest income quintile rose to the highest quintile.

Educational Attainment

The levels of education adults have completed are highly correlated with the circumstances in which they grew up. These outcomes result from differences all along the path from K–12 through undergraduate and graduate education. At each step, those from low-income backgrounds, Black and Hispanic students, and those whose parents do not have college degrees are most likely to encounter obstacles that prevent them from progressing.

In 2019, when 38 percent of adults had no education beyond high school, 45 percent of Black adults and 59 percent of Hispanic adults were in this situation. At the other end of the educational continuum, 25 percent of Asian adults and 15 percent of White adults had completed master's, doctoral, or professional degrees, compared with 10 percent of Black adults and 6 percent of Hispanic adults who had reached this level (table 3.1).

The racial gap in high school graduation has declined over time. In 1950, more than two and half times as many White adults as Black adults had completed high school—36 percent versus 14 percent. By 1980, that ratio had fallen to 1.4 and in 2019, when 95 percent of White and 89 percent of Black adults had completed high school, it was 1.1. The share of Black adults holding bachelor's degrees rose from 2 percent in 1950 to 8 percent in 1980 and to 26 percent in 2019. The increase for White adults over these years was from 7 percent to 18 percent to 40 percent. The ratio of the share of White to the share of Black adults with bachelor's degrees fell from 3.5 to 2.3 to 1.5 over these years (table 3.2). Yet while the share of Black adults with bachelor's

TABLE 3.1. Educational Attainment of Adults Ages 25 and Over, by Race and Ethnicity 2019

Smaller shares of Black and Hispanic adults than of White and Asian adults have completed at least a bachelor's degree.

	All	White	Black	Asian	Hispanic
Less than HS	10%	6%	12%	9%	28%
HS (including GED)	28%	27%	33%	18%	31%
Some college	16%	16%	19%	9%	14%
Associate	10%	11%	11%	7%	8%
Bachelor's	23%	25%	17%	33%	13%
Advanced degree	13%	15%	10%	25%	6%

Source: U.S. Census Bureau, Educational Attainment in the United States, 2020, table 3.

TABLE 3.2. Educational Attainment over Time by Race and Ethnicity

Both the share of Black adults who have completed high school and the share who have completed a bachelor's degree have risen relative to the share of White adults with these levels of education—but the absolute gap in college attainment has grown.

	Completed High School			Completed Bachelor's Degree			HS	BA
	All	White	Black	All	White	Black	White/ Black	White/ Black
1950	34%	36%	14%	6%	7%	2%	2.6	3.5
1960	41%	43%	22%	8%	8%	4%	2	2.0
1970	55%	57%	36%	11%	12%	6%	1.6	2.0
1980	69%	72%	51%	17%	18%	8%	1.4	2.3
1990	78%	81%	66%	21%	23%	11%	1.2	2.1
2000	84%	88%	79%	26%	28%	17%	1.1	1.6
2010	87%	92%	85%	30%	33%	20%	1.1	1.7
2019	90%	95%	89%	36%	40%	26%	1.1	1.5

Source: U.S. Department of Education, Digest of Education Statistics, 2019, table 104.10.

degrees has grown faster than that of Whites, from a very low base, it is also the case that the gap in the share of Whites and Blacks with bachelor's degrees has continued to grow, from 5 percentage points in 1950 to 14 points today (figure 3.3).

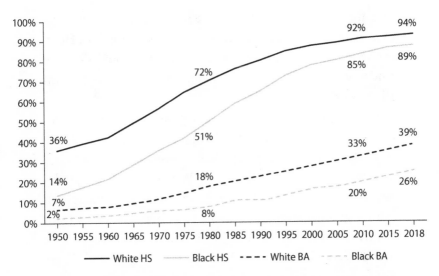

FIGURE 3.3. Share of Adults Who Have Completed High School and Who Have Completed Bachelor's Degrees
The racial gap in high school has narrowed, but the gap in bachelor's degree completion has not.

Note: High school graduates include those who earned GED or other equivalence degrees.
Source: U.S. Department of Education, *Digest of Education Statistics, 2019,* table 104.10.

Educational Pathways: High School Graduation and College Enrollment

These differences in the eventual educational attainment of high school students depend in part on college enrollment rates. But college enrollment rates are usually measured as the share of high school graduates who go on to college. These figures actually understate the gaps, because of differences in high school graduation rates.

Just over half of the young people who graduated from high school in 1969 enrolled in college the following year. Fifty years later, the share going straight to college had risen to 69 percent.

The most rapid growth was in the first two decades, but the increase in college participation rates has continued. However, the stories of different racial and ethnic groups—and of students from different family income backgrounds—are not all the same.

In 1980 the share of Hispanic high school graduates who enrolled immediately in college was similar to the share of White students who followed this path. However, between 1980 and 2018, the college continuation rate of White students rose gradually from 52 percent to 70 percent. The share of Hispanic high school graduates going straight to college declined from 50 percent in 1980 to 42 percent in 1986, before rising to 63 percent in 2018. Black high school graduates enroll at a significantly lower rate than White students, with the gap fluctuating between 4 and 18 percentage points—and Asian students consistently go on to college at the highest rates (figure 3.4).[1]

This is the picture for those who completed high school. How does considering high school graduation rates change this picture? In 2017–18, when 85 percent of the students who began high school four years earlier graduated with regular diplomas, 79 percent of Black and 81 percent of Hispanic students completed high school. In contrast, the graduation rates were 89 percent for White and 94 percent for Asian and Pacific Islander high school students (figure 3.5).[2]

Combining the differences in high school graduation rates with the differences in the continuation rate from high school graduation to college entry completes the story. The 70 percent continuation rate for White high school graduates implies that

1. Because of small sample sizes and volatility in the data, percentages are based on three-year moving averages.

2. U.S. Department of Education, *Digest of Education Statistics, 2018*, table 219.46.

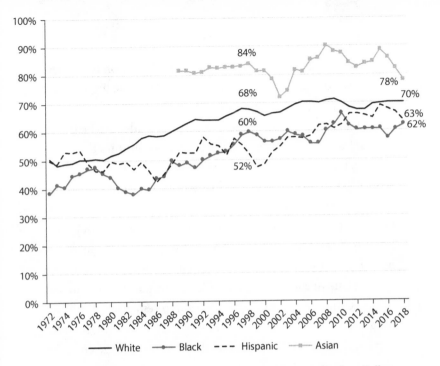

FIGURE 3.4. Share of High School Graduates Continuing Immediately to College, by Race and Ethnicity

Black high school graduates are less likely than others to enroll immediately in college.

Source: U.S. Department of Education, *Digest of Education Statistics, 2019*, table 302.20.

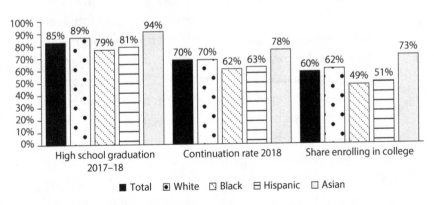

FIGURE 3.5. High School Graduation and College Enrollment Rates by Race/ Ethnicity

Differences in high school graduation rates increase the gaps in the shares of young people from different racial and ethnic groups going to college.

Source: U.S. Department of Education, *Digest of Education Statistics, 2018*, tables 219.46, 302.20.

62 percent of those who began high school went on to college. Lower continuation rates for Black and Hispanic high school graduates create larger gaps in college enrollment for all high school students. While 73 percent of Asian students who began high school graduated in four years and went immediately to college, for Black students, who combine a relatively low high school graduation rate with a low continuation rate for those who do complete high school, only 49 percent of those who began high school wound up going directly to college. So roughly three-fifths of White and three-quarters of Asians are in college the year after scheduled high school graduation; the same is true of a little over half of Hispanic and fewer than half of Black students. These facts are a sharp reminder of how far we are as a country from providing young people of different races and ethnicities with an equal chance for college entry, let alone college success.

Family Income and College Attendance

High school graduates from the top quintile of the family income distribution enroll in college at higher rates than those from middle- and lower-income families. In 2016, two-thirds of students from the lowest family income quintile and from the two middle-income quintiles continued on to college in the year following high school graduation. In contrast, 83 percent of those from the most affluent families enrolled in college immediately after high school. These gaps have narrowed somewhat over time. From 1978 to 1995, the gap between the shares of high- and low-income high school graduates going straight to college was almost always 35 percentage points or more. Between 1997 and 2016, the gap averaged about 27 points—falling below 20 points in 2015 and 2016. The gap between higher- and middle-income students has

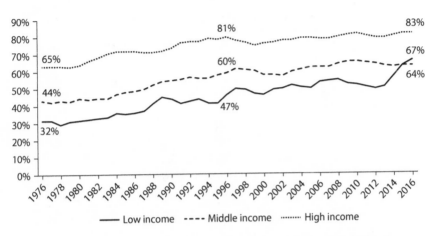

FIGURE 3.6. Share of High School Graduates Enrolling Immediately in College by Family Income
High school graduates from high-income families are more likely than others to go straight to college.
Source: U.S. Department of Education, *Digest of Education Statistics, 2017*, table 302.30.

narrowed less, ranging between 22 and 25 points between 1985 and 1987 and between 17 and 20 points between 2003 and 2016 (figure 3.6).

Notably, in recent years, low-income high school graduates have enrolled in college at higher rates than their middle-income peers. At least some of this pattern is attributable to differences in high school graduation rates: low-income students are less likely to finish high school than others but those who do get through are a little more likely than middle-income students to start college. For example, between 2006 and 2016, on average 7.2 percent of tenth to twelfth graders from the lowest family income quartile dropped out of school each year. Dropout rates are lower for students from the upper half of the income distribution (table 3.3).

TABLE 3.3. Annual Event Dropout Rate, 2006–16

High school dropout rates are highest for students from
low-income families.

Average	Share Dropping Out
Lowest quarter	7.2%
Middle-low quarter	5.3%
Middle-high quarter	3.6%
Highest quarter	3.9%

Source: U.S. Department of Education, *Digest of Education
Statistics, 2017*, table 219.57.

College Completion

Of the students who began college in 2011–12, 56 percent had
earned a credential by 2017; 12 percent were still enrolled, and
32 percent had left school without a degree or certificate. The
outcomes of students who begin college are closely correlated
with family backgrounds.

Leaving school without a credential is most common among
students whose parents have not completed college. Among
students who began college in 2011–12, the frequency of this
outcome ranged from 40 percent of those whose parents had
not completed high school and 43 percent of those whose parents had high school diplomas to 22 percent of those whose
parents' highest degree was a bachelor's degree and 12 percent
of those whose parents had professional degrees.

Students with highly educated parents were most likely to
earn bachelor's degrees: 20 percent of those whose parents'
highest level of education was a high school diploma had earned
bachelor's degrees by 2017; 53 percent of those whose parents'
highest degree was a bachelor's degree and 70 percent of those
whose parents held professional degrees had earned bachelor's
degrees (table 3.4).

TABLE 3.4. Postsecondary Outcomes across Demographic Groups for Students Beginning College in 2011–12

Students whose parents do not have a college education are more likely than others to leave school without a credential. They are also more likely to earn certificates or associate degrees rather than bachelor's degrees.

Parents' Highest Level of Education	Bachelor's Degree	Associate Degree	Certificate	No Degree, Enrolled	No Degree, Not Enrolled
All	37%	11%	9%	12%	32%
Do not know either parent's education level	13%	12%	15%	16%	44%
Did not complete high school	16%	15%	14%	15%	40%
High school diploma or equivalent	20%	11%	12%	13%	43%
Vocational/technical training	23%	13%	14%	12%	37%
Associate degree	30%	14%	8%	12%	36%
Some college but no degree	30%	13%	9%	12%	35%
Bachelor's degree	53%	9%	5%	11%	22%
Master's degree or equivalent	62%	8%	3%	9%	17%
Doctoral degree— professional practice	70%	3%	4%	10%	12%
Doctoral degree— research/scholarship	69%	5%	3%	11%	13%

Source: U.S. Department of Education, *Beginning Postsecondary Students Longitudinal Study, 2012/17.*

Pathways to College Attainment: A Closer Look

Enrolling in college is just one step on the path to earning a college degree. Final educational attainment is even more closely associated with family background than are the individual steps along the path toward that goal, as the differences compound. The U.S. Department of Education undertook an intensive longitudinal study of a large, randomly selected cohort of 2002 high school sophomores with whom they have since followed up several times. Although these data are now a little old, and the numbers are a bit different from the more recent data cited above, they provide us with a richer picture of pathways to college attainment for this Millennial cohort than we can obtain for other years. What follows draws on that data set.

Going to college but not completing a credential—the outcome for one-third of 2002 high school sophomores—is more common than not enrolling at all. This event was most common among Black and Hispanic students, those from low-income families, and those whose parents left high school or college without completing the programs they began. Among all groups, starting college but not graduating was much more common than not enrolling in college at all (table 3.5). This makes exploring the factors leading up to college enrollment that contribute to both the selection of a college and preparation to succeed there critical. It also raises obvious questions about the support students receive once they are enrolled.

Gaps in bachelor's degree completion rates conceal a range of differences in the educational paths of students from different backgrounds. Groups with the lowest bachelor's degree attainment rates are more likely than others to have earned undergraduate certificates or associate degrees. More than half of the credentials earned by Black and Hispanic students, by those from the lowest-income families, and by those whose parents had no more than a high school diploma were sub-baccalaureate credentials.

In other words, the gaps across groups in earning any degree or certificate are smaller than the gaps in bachelor's degree attainment. Almost four times as many students from the highest-income families as from the lowest-income families earned bachelor's degrees (67 percent versus 18 percent; see table 3.5). About twice as many earned a postsecondary credential

TABLE 3.5. Educational Pathways of 2002 High School Sophomores

The educational outcomes of high school students are highly correlated with race and ethnicity, family income, and parents' education level.

	Did Not Graduate from High School	Graduated from High School but Did Not Go to College	Went to College but Did Not Complete a Credential	Completed a Certificate or Associate Degree	Completed a Bachelor's Degree or Higher
Total	3%	13%	32%	19%	33%
Race/Ethnicity					
Asian, Hawaii/Pacific Islander, (4%)	2%	7%	28%	14%	50%
Black (14%)	5%	13%	40%	22%	20%
Hispanic (16%)	7%	15%	39%	21%	19%
Other (5%)	4%	19%	33%	18%	26%
White (60%)	2%	12%	29%	18%	40%
Family income					
$25,000 or less (21%)	7%	19%	36%	20%	18%
$25,001–$50,000 (32%)	3%	15%	35%	21%	25%
$50,001–$75,000 (21%)	2%	10%	32%	19%	36%
$75,001–$100,000 (13%)	1%	7%	27%	18%	47%
$100,001–$200,000 (10%)	0%	4%	24%	11%	61%
$200,001 or more (3%)	1%	3%	18%	11%	67%
Parents' highest level of education					
Did not finish high school (6%)	11%	20%	36%	21%	11%
Graduated from high school or GED (21%)	5%	21%	33%	22%	19%
Attended 2-year school, no degree (11%)	3%	16%	36%	23%	23%
Graduated from 2-year school (11%)	2%	12%	35%	24%	27%
Attended college, no 4-year degree (11%)	2%	12%	40%	18%	28%
Graduated from college (22%)	2%	7%	30%	16%	46%
Completed master's degree (11%)	1%	5%	24%	11%	59%
Completed PhD, MD, other advanced degree (5%)	0%	3%	23%	12%	60%

Source: U.S. Department of Education, *Education Longitudinal Study of 2002.* Calculations by the authors.

(79 percent versus 38 percent). Focusing only on bachelor's degrees makes the gaps appear larger. But understanding the inequality in college outcomes requires examining not just whether students go to college but where they go, whether they complete their programs, and what kinds of programs they complete. Tables 3.4 and 3.5 provide a striking reminder of one of the central themes of this book: the powerful impact the education parents have in this unequal society has on their children's educational prospects. To interrupt the spiral of inequality requires sustained attention to improving the next generation's educational opportunities right from the start of their lives.

Even within family income groups, Black and Hispanic students are much less likely than White and Asian students to complete bachelor's degrees within eight years of their expected high school graduation date. The racial and ethnic gaps in completing any postsecondary credential are smaller but follow a similar pattern (table 3.6).

Stratification within Higher Education

Some of the differences in postsecondary outcomes are associated with the types of institutions in which students enroll. The sorting of students by type of institutions—and the resource levels associated with these institutions—is behind much of the concern over the relationship between higher education and the perpetuation of socioeconomic status.

Going to college can mean very different things. Children growing up in affluent families vie for scarce places in a small number of highly selective private nonprofit and public flagship institutions. The disproportionate number of newspaper and magazine articles about competitive college admissions might suggest that applying to college always means intensive preparation for the SAT and/or ACT standardized admissions tests

TABLE 3.6. Educational Attainment of 2004 High School Graduates by Family Income and Race/Ethnicity

Black and Hispanic high school graduates are less likely than White and Asian students from families with similar incomes to complete bachelor's degrees.

	Bachelor's Degree within 8 Years					
	All income	$25,000 or less	$25,001–$50,000	$50,001–$75,000	$75,001–$100,000	$100,001 or more
White	40%	21%	29%	39%	50%	65%
Black	20%	14%	16%	28%	39%	36%
Hispanic	19%	12%	18%	20%	27%	49%
Asian	50%	37%	48%	52%	59%	69%
Other	26%	15%	17%	33%	32%	66%
	Any Postsecondary Credential within 8 Years					
White	58%	38%	51%	58%	68%	74%
Black	42%	37%	40%	46%	56%	60%
Hispanic	40%	35%	36%	49%	45%	67%
Asian	64%	54%	63%	65%	72%	NA
Other	44%	34%	34%	52%	55%	NA

Source: U.S. Department of Education, Education Longitudinal Study of 2002. Calculations by the authors.

and anxious waiting for verdicts from schools that reject far more qualified applicants than they accept. But the reality is that for most students, applying to college means locating one or two colleges near home and registering at an institution that accepts most or all of the high school graduates seeking the opportunity.

Students from different backgrounds sort into very different institutions. Overall, half of students beginning college in 2011–12 first enrolled in a public or private nonprofit four-year college or university; 38 percent started at a community college. But the share starting in four-year institutions ranged from 44 percent of the lowest-income students to more than three-quarters of those from families in the top quarter of the income distribution. Similarly, Black and Hispanic students

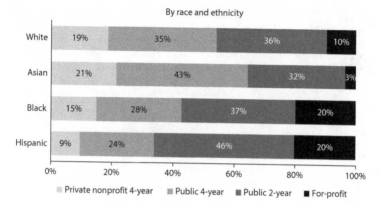

FIGURE 3.7a. Sectors of Initial College Enrollment
Black and Hispanic students are less likely than White and Asian students to enroll in public and private nonprofit four-year institutions; Black and Hispanic students are more likely than others to attend for-profit institutions.

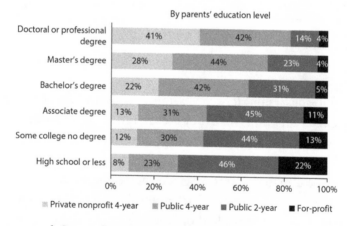

FIGURE 3.7b. Sectors of Initial College Enrollment
College students whose parents do not have college degrees are more likely than others to enroll in public two-year and for-profit institutions.

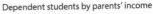

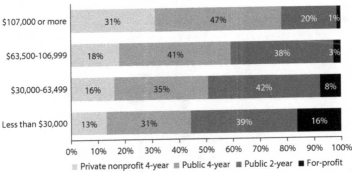

FIGURE 3.7c. Sectors of Initial College Enrollment
College students from low-income families are more likely than others to enroll in public two-year and for-profit institutions.

Source: U.S. Department of Education, *Beginning Postsecondary Students Longitudinal Study,* 2012/17. Calculations by the authors.

and those whose parents have relatively low levels of education were less likely than others to enroll in public and private nonprofit four-year institutions—and more likely to go to community colleges or for-profit institutions (figure 3.7).

In other words, stratification of students within higher education looks similar whether categorizing students by race and ethnicity, by their parents' education level, or by the incomes of their families of origin—and reinforces the differences in college enrollment rates between groups. White and Asian students, those whose parents have at least a four-year degree, and those from relatively high-income families are most likely to enroll in private nonprofit and public four-year colleges and universities. Black and Hispanic students, those whose parents are not four-year college graduates, and those from lower-income families are most likely to enroll in public two-year and for-profit institutions.

The next layer of stratification occurs within four-year public and private nonprofit institutions, where larger shares of Asian

TABLE 3.7. Four-Year College Students by Institutional Selectivity, 2015–16

Students from high-income families are mostly likely to attend very selective four-year institutions; those from low-income families are most likely to attend minimally selective or open admissions institutions.

	Very Selective	Moderately Selective	Minimally Selective or Open Admissions
Lowest quintile	10%	52%	38%
Second quintile	13%	59%	28%
Third quintile	11%	63%	26%
Fourth quintile	21%	58%	21%
Highest quintile	29%	61%	11%

Source: U.S. Department of Education, National Postsecondary Student Aid Study, 2016. Calculations by the authors.
Note: Income quintiles are based on 2014 income: Lowest = $29,100 or less; Second = $29,101–$52,697; Third = $52,698–$82,033; Fourth = $82,034–$129,006; Highest = $129,007 or higher.

and White students and smaller shares of Black and Hispanic students attend highly selective institutions. The share of students attending selective institutions increases with both family income and parents' education level. For example, 90 percent of students from families from the highest income quintile of the population who attended public or private nonprofit four-year institutions were enrolled in moderately or highly selective institutions, compared with 62 percent of those from the lowest family income quintile and 74 percent of those from the middle quintile (table 3.7).

Some of the differences in the types of institutions in which students from different backgrounds enroll are associated with differences in academic achievement levels—which, as detailed in chapter 4, are highly correlated with the environments in which children grow up. Students with high school GPAs below 3.5 or SAT scores below 1200 rarely attend very selective colleges and universities. Those with strong academic credentials are much less likely than others to enroll in open admission four-year institutions or institutions offering only shorter-term programs (table 3.8).

These academic qualifications are not equally distributed across demographic groups. For example, the share of 2015–16 college students with a high school GPA of 3.5 or higher ranged from 32 percent of those from the lowest family income quartile to 53 percent of those from the highest quartile. Forty percent of White students and 41 percent of Asian students had GPAs this high, compared with 21 percent of Black and 27 percent of Hispanic students. GPAs were also correlated with parents' highest level of education, with the shares with GPAs of 3.5 or higher ranging from 24 percent of the children whose parents lacked a high school diploma and 26 percent of the children of high school graduates to 46 percent and 48 percent, respectively, of those whose parents held professional and doctoral degrees.

The pattern is similar for test scores. The only groups in which 5 percent or more of college students scored above 1400 on the SAT were those from the highest family income quartile, Asian students, and those whose parents held advanced degrees (table 3.9).

Nonetheless, even among students with similar high school records and test scores, those from lower socioeconomic backgrounds and Black and Hispanic students are less likely than others to attend moderately or very selective colleges and universities. For example, the share of students with a high school GPA of 3.5 or higher who enroll in very selective institutions ranges from 18 percent of those from the lowest family income quartile to 34 percent of those from the highest income quartile. Among those with SAT scores of 1400 or higher, the share enrolling in either moderately or very selective institutions ranges from 25 percent of Black students and 38 percent of Hispanic students to 78 percent of White students and 89 percent of Asian students with these test scores (table 3.10).

TABLE 3.8. Academic Achievement and College Selectivity

Students with high test scores and high school grades attend more selective institutions than do other students.

	All (with GPA)	High School GPA				All (with SAT or ACT)	SAT or Equivalent				
		Less than 2.0 (4%)	2.0–2.9 (29%)	3.0–3.4 (33%)	3.5 or higher (34%)		800 or lower (17%)	801–1000 (36%)	1001–1200 (31%)	1201–1400 (13%)	1401 or higher (3%)
Very selective	11%	3%	4%	8%	22%	13%	3%	6%	14%	31%	53%
Moderately selective	33%	14%	23%	34%	42%	35%	20%	35%	44%	38%	20%
Minimally selective	4%	5%	5%	4%	4%	4%	6%	5%	4%	3%	2%
Open admission	10%	13%	13%	11%	7%	9%	13%	11%	8%	5%	7%
Not a four-year institution	42%	64%	56%	43%	26%	38%	58%	43%	30%	23%	18%

Source: U.S. Department of Education, National Postsecondary Student Aid Study, 2016. Calculations by the authors.

Note: Overall shares attending each type of institution differ for high school GPA and SAT or equivalent because not all students report GPA and not all students take admissions tests.

TABLE 3.9. Academic Achievement by Socioeconomic Background

Academic credentials are highly correlated with family background.

	High School GPA				SAT or Equivalent				
	Less than 2.0 (4%)	2.0–2.9 (29%)	3.0–3.4 (33%)	3.5 or higher (34%)	800 or lower (17%)	801–1000 (36%)	1001–1200 (31%)	1201–1400 (13%)	1401 or higher (3%)
Less than $27,900	4%	30%	34%	32%	27%	40%	23%	8%	1%
$27,900–62,999	3%	26%	34%	37%	19%	39%	29%	11%	2%
$63,000–113,499	2%	21%	32%	45%	11%	35%	37%	14%	3%
$113,500 or more	1%	16%	30%	53%	6%	25%	39%	24%	6%
White	4%	24%	32%	40%	10%	34%	36%	17%	3%
Asian	3%	23%	32%	41%	12%	30%	32%	18%	8%
Black	5%	40%	33%	21%	34%	40%	19%	5%	1%
Hispanic	5%	34%	34%	27%	24%	42%	25%	8%	1%
Less than HS	7%	38%	32%	24%	28%	42%	23%	6%	1%
HS	6%	35%	33%	26%	24%	41%	24%	8%	2%
Vocational training	6%	34%	33%	28%	19%	39%	30%	10%	2%
Some college, no degree	5%	31%	35%	29%	20%	40%	29%	9%	2%
Associate	5%	31%	34%	30%	18%	41%	30%	10%	2%
Bachelor's	4%	25%	32%	39%	13%	34%	34%	16%	3%
Master's	3%	23%	32%	43%	11%	32%	35%	17%	5%
Professional	3%	23%	28%	46%	10%	27%	33%	23%	7%
Doctoral	3%	18%	31%	48%	9%	21%	36%	24%	10%

Source: U.S. Department of Education, *National Postsecondary Student Aid Study, 2016.* Calculations by the authors.

TABLE 3.10. College Selectivity by Demographic Groups for High-Achieving Students

Among college students with strong academic credentials, Asian and White students, those from affluent families, and those whose parents have high levels of education are more likely than others to attend selective institutions.

	GPA 3.0–3.4		GPA 3.5 or Higher		SAT 1201–1400		SAT 1400 or Higher	
	Very selective	Very or moderately selective	Very selective	Very or moderately selective	Very selective	Very or moderately selective	Very selective	Very or moderately selective
All	8%	42%	22%	64%	31%	69%	53%	72%
Dependent students' parents' income								
Less than $27,900	7%	38%	18%	54%	30%	61%	49%	65%
$27,900–62,999	8%	47%	20%	65%	30%	69%	49%	70%
$63,000–113,499	8%	50%	22%	71%	33%	80%	56%	87%
$113,500 or more	16%	68%	34%	82%	43%	86%	72%	91%
Race/Ethnicity								
White	9%	46%	21%	69%	30%	74%	51%	78%
Black	6%	40%	16%	56%	24%	44%	18%	25%
Hispanic	6%	32%	18%	47%	24%	45%	32%	38%
Asian	18%	48%	40%	71%	47%	74%	81%	89%

Parents' highest education level							NA	NA
Did not complete high school	7%	28%	14%	43%	23%	35%	NA	NA
High school diploma or equivalent	5%	29%	14%	48%	16%	40%	29%	39%
Vocational/technical training	5%	33%	13%	49%	21%	54%	20%	26%
Associate degree	5%	34%	15%	57%	18%	56%	39%	51%
Some college, no degree	6%	38%	13%	55%	19%	56%	23%	49%
Bachelor's degree	9%	50%	23%	69%	33%	75%	49%	78%
Master's degree	12%	54%	28%	74%	38%	80%	64%	83%
Professional degree	15%	55%	42%	82%	47%	87%	83%	99%
Doctoral degree	21%	62%	39%	78%	47%	77%	75%	90%

Source: U.S. Department of Education, *National Postsecondary Student Aid Study, 2016.* Calculations by the authors.
Note: Based on NCES definition of selectivity, which relies on IPEDS data. Incorporates the share of applicants admitted and the 25th and 75th percentiles of SAT/ACT scores.

Enrollment in very selective institutions is similar among the three lower-income quartiles within similar GPA and test score groups, but those from families with incomes of $113,500 or more are much more likely to be enrolled in these institutions. Focusing on moderately and very selective institutions combined, the enrollment rate rises steadily with income. For example, among students with GPA of 3.5 or higher, about 20 percent from each of the lower three income groups attended very selective institutions, compared with 34 percent of those from the highest-income group. Attendance at either a very or moderately selective institution rose from 54 percent to 65 percent to 71 percent to 82 percent moving up the income scale.

Asian students are much more likely than White students with similar academic achievement levels to attend very selective institutions. For example, 81 percent of Asian and 51 percent of White students with test scores over 1400 are at these institutions. However, the contrast at moderately or very selective institutions is between 25 percent of Black and 38 percent of Hispanic students with these high scores—and 78 percent of White and 89 percent of Asian students.

In other words, even very highly qualified Black and Hispanic students, as well as those from low SES backgrounds, are much less likely than others with their qualifications to enroll in the selective institutions at which they would have had a good chance of acceptance. Many factors contribute to this reality. A central problem is that many low-income students do not apply to selective institutions.[3] They may not know that which college they attend could make a significant difference; they may be focused on staying close to home or going to the

3. Hoxby and Avery, "The Missing 'One-Offs.'"

same institutions as their friends; or they may believe that they would be out of place at a very selective institution. Another issue is that they likely believe that the higher published tuition prices of more selective institutions put them out of reach. In fact, because well-endowed institutions generally have more generous need-based aid than others—and because they enroll relatively small shares of high-need students—the net prices students from low-income households pay are typically lowest at the most selective colleges and universities.

Does This Stratification Matter?

These enrollment patterns would matter less if completion rates were unrelated to the institutions students attend and if all bachelor's degrees carried equal weight in the labor market. But there is strong evidence that it matters where students—particularly those from disadvantaged backgrounds—attend college. Students who attend more selective colleges with more resources to invest in them are more likely than their peers to graduate and they tend to have higher post-college earnings. The fact that first-generation and low-income students are less likely than others to apply to and enroll in these institutions decreases their chances for upward mobility.

Post-college earnings are certainly not the only measure of post-college success. But they are the most commonly and reliably available. Moreover, a major question posed by researchers investigating differential outcomes across institutions relates to whether or not it is worth paying for a more elite institution. In fact, as noted above, although these colleges and universities generally have higher published tuition prices than less selective institutions, they tend to charge low-income students lower net prices because of their generous need-based aid policies.[4] So it is frequently students from more affluent families, who are eligible for less need-based aid, who actually face the question of whether or not to pay more for a more elite school.

Measuring earnings differentials is complicated by the different characteristics of the student bodies at institutions of different "quality"—however defined. By definition, students who graduate from highly selective institutions come to college with characteristics that make them more likely than others to do well in college and to succeed in the labor market. They did well in high school, have high test scores, worked hard to develop outstanding résumés so they would be accepted at the school of their choice, and display ambition to succeed. So, it is not enough to compare their earnings to the earnings of graduates of less selective institutions—who did not enter college with the same qualifications. Even sophisticated statistical analyses cannot totally eliminate the problem of distinguishing the impact of the college attended from the impact of students' characteristics. But the majority of attempts to tackle this problem have concluded that there is a significant earnings payoff to attending a more selective college.

The widely publicized work of two prominent economists challenges this overall conclusion from other studies but confirms the importance of selectivity for low-income and underrepresented students. Stacy Dale and Alan Krueger, focusing only on a group of thirty selective colleges and universities, compared the earnings of students who had been admitted to approximately the same set of colleges but had made different enrollment choices. They did not find a significant overall payoff to selectivity—but they did find that low-income students who

4. Baum and Lee, *Understanding Endowments*.

graduated from more-selective institutions earned more than similar students who attended less selective institutions.[5] In later research focusing on the same limited set of colleges and universities, the same authors found that controlling for the set of schools to which students applied significantly reduced the measured earnings payoff to attending a highly selective institution. Again, the results were different for Black and Hispanic students and those whose parents had low levels of education.[6]

Discussions that cite this work as support for the idea that it is not worth paying for a more selective college miss the important finding that selectivity does have a significant impact on later earnings for students from less-privileged backgrounds. They also ignore the fact that the "less selective" institutions in the study are actually among the most selective colleges and universities in the nation.

Moreover, most research on the subject concludes that while college quality has a different impact on different groups of students, there is a significant average earnings payoff to earning a bachelor's degree from a more selective institution. Studies have examined outcomes across public universities within one state, as well as using national samples. For example, a 2018 study from the Federal Reserve Bank of New York found that students who graduated from selective four-year colleges earned 11 percent more after six years than similar students who graduated from nonselective four-year colleges; the gap grew to 20 percent after ten years. Moreover, the earnings gaps associated with family income at the time of college enrollment were significantly smaller for the graduates of selective colleges than

5. Dale and Krueger, "Estimating the Payoff to Attending a More Selective College."
6. Dale and Krueger, "Estimating the Return to College Selectivity."

for those who attended less selective institutions.[7] In other words, attending a more selective college helped those from lower-income backgrounds "catch up" to their peers from more affluent families.

A 2017 study using nationally representative longitudinal data and controlling as much as possible for the differences in the characteristics of students attending colleges with different levels of selectivity found significant earnings differences ten years after graduation between each group of colleges and the group just below it in terms of selectivity.[8] A study in Texas that compared students who just made it through the admissions process at a flagship university to those with similar qualifications who did not quite make the cutoff and went to less selective universities found a 20 percent earnings gap between the two groups.[9]

The finding that the effect is largest for students from disadvantaged backgrounds appears in multiple studies. Some studies focus on outcomes other than earnings, such as the probability of attending graduate school, health, and marital stability.[10] The body of evidence on the subject points in a clear direction.

7. Chakrabarti and Jiang, "Education's Role in Earnings, Employment, and Economic Mobility."

8. Witteveen and Attewell, "The Earnings Payoff from Attending a Selective College."

9. Hoekstra, "The Effect of Attending the Flagship State University on Earnings." See also Black and Smith, "How Robust Is the Evidence on the Effects of College Quality?"; Black and Smith, "Estimating the Returns to College Quality."

10. Long, "Changes in the Returns to Education and College Quality"; Long, "College Quality and Early Adult Outcomes."

Undermatching

Understanding the negative impact of undermatching (attending less selective institutions than those to which students could likely be admitted) and focusing on the importance of supporting the enrollment of more low- and moderate-income students at selective colleges and universities is in no way inconsistent with urging upper-middle-class students to avoid obsessing over the idea that their success in life depends on being accepted to Harvard, Yale, or Princeton. A student from a relatively privileged background who ends up at a flagship public university or a highly selective liberal arts college[11] should not despair—the differences in life outcomes among these institutions are not significant for students who arrive with substantial social capital (broad experiences, connections to educated adults who can provide guidance, a sense of belonging) and graduate with resources and connections that will help them get established in their careers.

The question of whether a first-generation student, whose parents have no experience with higher education or connections in the professional world and who has not grown up expecting to get ahead financially, professionally, and socially, goes to a selective college or university rather than to a community college or a for-profit institution—or even a broad-access regional public institution—is entirely different. The issue here is not how far down the ranking in *U.S. News* the admissions process has forced the student. The issue is whether well-prepared low-income students—for whom all of the evidence indicates institutional resources and selectivity significantly affect

---

11. See Bruni, "How to Survive the College Admissions Madness."

outcomes—have the opportunity to attend colleges and universities most likely to support their success.

Conclusion

Young people from different socioeconomic backgrounds have starkly different postsecondary educational experiences and outcomes. Black and Hispanic students, those from low-income households, and those whose parents do not have college degrees are less likely to graduate from high school, less likely to go to college, less likely to go to four-year public and private nonprofit institutions—particularly selective colleges and universities—if they do continue their education, less likely to complete college credentials, and, if they do graduate, less likely to earn bachelor's degrees.

These patterns mean that the gaps in life prospects between those who grow up with privilege and those who do not are more visible after the college years than before. The chapters that follow look back to the earlier life experiences and circumstances that shape students' college opportunities and forward to the consequences of those differing postsecondary experiences and outcomes for their later lives.

CHAPTER 4

Getting to the College Door: Inequality in Pre-College Circumstances and Experiences

As we have just seen, differences in the postsecondary experiences of people from different socioeconomic and racial/ethnic backgrounds are dramatic. Chapter 3 reminds us that young people from relatively high-income backgrounds are much more likely than others to enroll in college when they graduate from high school. Black high school graduates enroll at much lower rates than those from other racial and ethnic groups. Moreover, those who do go on to college enroll in very different types of institutions. The share attending four-year public and private nonprofit colleges and universities increases with family income, as does the share within those institutions enrolling in doctoral universities. Older students and Black students are much more likely than others to enroll in the for-profit sector. Both completion rates among those who begin college and the highest levels of educational attainment among adults are similarly associated with family background and with race and ethnicity.

Postsecondary institutions and the public policies determining funding both for institutions and for students could do more than they now do to diminish these outcome gaps. But the fundamental problems of inequality in postsecondary education originate at a much earlier point in the lives of potential college students. Young adults from different backgrounds are in very different circumstances when they reach the point of enrolling in college—or pause or end their education in favor of alternative pathways.

On average, children from low-income families, those whose parents do not have a college education, and Black and Hispanic children grow up without many of the resources and experiences in and out of school that prepare others to enroll and succeed in college. Parents with very limited resources cannot provide their children with the same learning activities, experiences, and other forms of enrichment enjoyed by those in more affluent households. Living in inadequate housing in dangerous and underresourced neighborhoods has a long-lasting impact on children's development. Limited access to health and dental care makes it harder for children to learn. And the schools in low-income and segregated neighborhoods rarely offer the same learning environments as those in affluent largely White neighborhoods.

As long as these realities persist, it will be unrealistic to expect that changes to higher education alone have the potential to eliminate—or even come close to eliminating—the current gaps. In this chapter, we review the evidence about the impact on children of differences in parental resources and education levels, neighborhoods and housing, health care, and K–12 school-ing. We rely heavily on *Whither Opportunity*, an ambitious com-pendium of research on these issues, published in 2011 by the Russell Sage Foundation and the Spencer Foundation. Our goal is not to provide a comprehensive literature review but to sum-marize key findings from rigorous research. We do not attempt systematically to evaluate potential solutions to the serious prob-lems we describe. Rather, our intent is to focus attention on the barriers facing many people seeking, as young adults or later in life, to improve their lives through postsecondary education. It is vital that advocates and policymakers take account of these bar-riers and tackle them through evidence-based public policy—even while pursuing reforms within higher education to improve outcomes for those who come to the college door in need of par-ticular supports.

A Theoretical Framework

James Heckman, who won a Nobel prize in economics for path-breaking advances in the highly mathematical field of economic statistics, has done convincing work on the importance of early childhood education and cognitive and social development. His concept of "dynamic complementarity," or learning begets learn-ing, is central to understanding how higher education can best contribute to mitigating inequality. The basic idea is that people with strong backgrounds in learning go on to learn more easily than others. Children learn how to learn. Those who have not had early learning opportunities struggle to take advantage of later opportunities. Even if everyone had access to the same college opportunities, people from more privileged backgrounds—who had stronger learning environments both in school and out of school during their childhood—would get more value added from those experiences, widening the inequality of outcomes.[1]

Heckman argues that early interventions can be much more productive than those later in life: "Life cycle skill formation is dynamic in nature. Skill begets skill; motivation begets motivation. If a child is not motivated and stimulated to learn and engage early on in life, the more likely it is that when the child becomes an adult, it will fail in social and economic life."[2]

The policy implications that flow from this model are in tension with prevailing practices. Cunha and Heckman compare a policy with large and effective investment in early education with one that limits early investment and attempts to compensate with late adolescent investments including adolescent literacy, mentoring, and subsidized college tuition. The second is much more expensive than the first for comparable results. Moreover, if investment is made in early education, the productivity of those later investments is much greater. Thus, it is early experiences and the associated social and emotional development, in addition to cognitive development, that contribute most to differences in the college success of young people from different socioeconomic backgrounds.[3]

Poverty and Income Inequality

Unlike the gaps between Black children and White children, which declined in the 1970s and have been stable since, the gap in achievement between children from high- and low-income families has grown over time and is about 50 percent larger than

1. Heckman and Schultz, "Invest in the Very Young."
2. Heckman, "Schools, Skills, and Synapses."
3. Cuhna and Heckman, "The Technology of Skill Formation."

it was forty years ago.[4] The achievement levels of low-income children have risen over time, but those of higher-income children have risen more rapidly.[5] The gap is already large when children enter kindergarten, and it remains fairly steady through the school years.

According to Sean Reardon, rising inequality probably contributes to the growth in the gap but is not the whole explanation. Even looking only at families above the median, the association between income and achievement levels is growing, so the issue is not just poverty or severe deprivation. The fact that the gaps across children whose parents have different levels of education have not grown at the same time as gaps by income levels suggests that money is a central part of the story.[6]

Not surprisingly, families with higher incomes spend more on their children than do others. They don't just live in more expensive houses, eat out more often, and buy nicer clothing. Some send their children to private schools; most spend a considerable amount on enrichment activities. Music lessons, summer camp, travel, and other experiences that help children expand their horizons (not to mention padding their college applications) all cost money. These expenditures contribute to the gaps in school readiness and, later, college readiness across young people from different socioeconomic backgrounds.

Not only the number of dollars but even the share of total family spending devoted to children's enrichment rises with income. A recent study found that expenditures on activities

4. Reardon, "The Widening Academic Achievement Gap between the Rich and the Poor."

5. Duncan and Murnane, "Rising Inequality in Family Incomes and Children's Educational Outcomes."

6. Reardon, "The Widening Academic Achievement Gap between the Rich and the Poor."

like art and music lessons, children's books, magazines, toys, sports equipment and lessons, tutoring, computers, trips, and electronics account for 3 percent ($610 in 2020 dollars) of the budgets of low-income families and 9 percent ($10,160) of the budgets for the 40 percent of families with the highest incomes. As an example, average annual expenditures per child on sports ranged from $120 for the lowest-income families to $990 for those in the top 20 percent. Families in the lowest income quintile spend just one-third of the amount spent by those in the second quintile and one-fifth of the amount spent by those in the third quintile, with the differences largest for expenditures on music lessons, travel, and summer camp.[7]

There are also striking differences in time-use patterns between low- and high-income families, especially time spent in "novel" places. Estimates suggest that between birth and age six, children from high-income families will have spent 1,300 more hours in novel contexts—places other than home, school, or the care of another parent or a day-care provider—than children from low-income families.[8]

Although the association between money and other family characteristics makes it difficult to distinguish the precise effects of each factor on gaps in school readiness and academic success, experimental studies indicate that more money makes a measurable difference, even given family structure, educational background, language use, and other circumstances. Income transfers to low-income families and increases in the Earned Income Tax Credit, which puts dollars in the pockets of

7. Kaushal, Magnuson, and Waldfogel, "How Is Family Income Related to Investments in Children's Learning?"

8. Phillips, "Parenting, Time Use, and Disparities in Academic Outcomes."

low-income families, show a significant impact on children's achievement levels.[9]

High-income families invest an increasing amount of time and resources into their children's cognitive development, and it is difficult for those with more limited resources to keep up. According to Annette Lareau, middle- and upper-class parents engage in "concerted cultivation," carefully managing the intellectual and socioemotional development of their children.[10]

These differences in the experiences of children from low- and high-income families contribute significantly to academic achievement gaps. One perspective on this issue comes from evidence that it is during the summer months—not the school year—that these gaps accumulate most for school-age children. These are the periods during which more-privileged children benefit from summer programs, books, and parents with the time and knowledge to engage them in substantive conversations.[11] Despite the inequalities in elementary and secondary school environments, schooling to some extent offsets these family and community influences. The gap in achievement between ninth-grade students from high and low SES backgrounds appears to result mainly from differences in summer learning over the elementary school years, reflecting unequal learning opportunities in children's home and community environments, while less-privileged students "hold their own" during the school year. These early out-of-school

9. Duncan and Murnane, "Rising Inequality in Family Incomes and Children's Educational Outcomes."

10. Lareau, *Unequal Childhoods.*

11. Mullainathan, "To Help Tackle Inequality, Remember the Advantages You've Had."

differences explain much of the differences in high school track placement, high school completion rates, and four-year college attendance.[12]

The combination of the increasing correlation between family income and academic achievement and the extent to which academic achievement predicts adult earnings exacerbates inequality and reduces economic mobility.[13]

Housing and Neighborhoods

Some children grow up in nice houses on tree-lined streets in communities with attentive adults, near well-equipped and safe parks, libraries, and good schools. Others grow up in economically depressed neighborhoods with boarded-up buildings, unsanitary conditions, substantial criminal activity, scarce and problematic adult supervision, and failing schools. It is impossible to imagine that these differences would fail to affect children's psychological health and attitudes toward learning.

Involvement in drugs, criminal activity, and teen childbirth obviously interfere with academic achievement. Lack of access to high-quality food and medical care because of geographical constraints affects physical health. Controlling for family income levels, young people who grow up in disadvantaged neighborhoods have lower high school graduation rates and lower levels of educational attainment than those growing up in more-privileged areas. These outcomes appear to be affected

12. Alexander, Entwisle, and Olson, "Lasting Consequences of the Summer Learning Gap."

13. Reardon, "The Widening Academic Achievement Gap between the Rich and the Poor."

by the quality of the schools and the characteristics of class-mates and by other characteristics of the neighborhoods.[14]

Where young children live has a significant impact on how ready to learn they are when they start kindergarten. Living con-ditions continue to directly affect their ability to succeed in school throughout the K–12 years. The quality of their housing—whether they are exposed to lead paint, have functioning bath-rooms, live with rodents, have privacy and quiet places—affects their physical health, their emotional development, and their parents' stress levels. The neighborhoods in which their homes are located—the level of violence, the employment status of adult neighbors, the presence of criminal activity, the available public resources—affect the people who influence them, the choices they make, and their ability to focus on learning. It should be no surprise that young people who grow up in low-quality housing and in disadvantaged neighborhoods reach their late teens less prepared than others to enroll and succeed in college.

Housing Quality

The environment in which children live can directly affect their physical health, which, as discussed in detail below, has a pro-found impact on academic achievement. Numerous studies have revealed a range of effects. Unsanitary and unsafe living condi-tions are associated with developmental delays, poor physical health, and behavioral problems.[15] Poor air quality, which gener-ates and exacerbates respiratory problems, negatively affects

---

14. Roy, Maynard, and Weiss, *The Hidden Costs of the Housing Crisis.*

15. Coley, Lynch, and Kull, "The Effects of Housing and Neighborhood Chaos on Children."

student test scores and school readiness.[16] Exposure to lead paint that leaves even low levels of lead in the blood reduces children's future test scores; lead poisoning may be one of the causes of gaps in educational attainment across socioeconomic groups.[17] Noisy and crowded housing conditions are associated with delayed cognitive development, lower reading skills, and behavioral adjustment problems. Both overcrowding and poor housing maintenance are associated with reduced high school graduation rates.[18]

It is not easy to isolate the impact of housing quality from other related aspects of growing up in a poor household. But many studies attempting to control for other factors do find that poor quality housing itself hurts children's prospects. For example, a study of children in Cleveland whose formative years coincided with the housing crisis between 2007 and 2010 revealed that those who experienced foreclosure or substandard housing were less prepared for school, had higher levels of lead in their blood, were subject to more mistreatment, and moved more often, controlling for other factors. The results of this study also indicated that eliminating housing and neighborhood disadvantage could significantly narrow the achievement gap between African American and White children.[19] In addition to obviously unhealthy circumstances such as rodent infestation, inadequate heat, and unsanitary conditions, overcrowding and noise can lead to cramped or inadequate study areas, preventing children from completing homework.[20] The coronavirus

16. Marcotte, "Something in the Air?"

17. Azier et al., "Do Low Levels of Blood Lead Reduce Children's Future Test Scores?"

18. Roy, Maynard, and Weiss, *The Hidden Costs of the Housing Crisis.*

19. Colton et al., "Temporal Effects of Distressed Housing."

20. Brennan, *The Positive Impacts of Affordable Housing on Education.*

pandemic and the widespread shift to at-home, online learning brought these unequal home learning environments to the fore and, no doubt, put the students living in these circumstances at even more severe disadvantage in terms of learning. The effects are likely to be long-lasting. Attention to inadequate conditions for learning, as well as other aspects of deprivation for lower-income families, has gone disproportionately to urban poverty. The pandemic served as a reminder that poor families in rural areas are also highly vulnerable to adverse circumstances for maintaining health and well-being.[21]

Despite overall improvements in housing quality over time, millions of households still live in severely or moderately inadequate housing, facing problems with plumbing, heating, electricity, and maintenance.[22] In 2013, almost 6 million households lived in these circumstances. Nine percent of Black households, 7 percent of Hispanic households, and 10 percent of households below the poverty level lived in such inadequate housing, compared with 5 percent of all households.[23]

Frequent Moves

Households that live in substandard housing and/or struggle to pay the rent are subject to frequent moves, including those resulting from eviction. There is conflicting evidence about how much frequent school changes affect academic achievement, but there is a clear consensus that high mobility rates have some negative effect for both the students who move and

---

21. Mueller et al., "Impacts of the COVID-19 Pandemic on Rural America."

22. Turner and Kingsley, *Federal Programs for Addressing Low-Income Housing Needs*; Kingsley, *Trends in Housing Problems*.

23. U.S. Census Bureau, American Community Survey, American Fact Finder.

their classmates. These issues affect children of all ages, from elementary school through high school. One study estimated that if Black children moved as infrequently as White children, the Black-White test gap would decline by 14 percent.[24]

A significant number of studies have found that moving frequently is detrimental for children's educational outcomes, reducing attendance, social and emotional adjustment, and academic performance and increasing grade retention and dropping out.[25] The conclusions of some of the studies examining the impact of frequent moves may be questionable because of the difficulty of controlling for other characteristics that are associated with high rates of mobility. These other factors may explain a significant share of the differences in outcomes. On the other hand, studies that examine the impact of changing schools without focusing on the reasons for those changes may understate the impact of forced moves because of housing problems—as opposed to moves motivated by the desire to attend a better school.[26] It seem seems clear that the effects of frequent switches in housing and schools are negative, particularly for children from low socioeconomic backgrounds.[27]

High levels of mobility also affect other children in the classroom because new children entering frequently require extra attention and resources. High rates of student mobility are associated with slower movement through the curriculum for entire classes, so students in these schools are not as far along as others and perform poorly on indicators of educational

24. Scanlon and Devine, "Residential Mobility and Youth Well-being."
25. Mueller and Tighe, "Making the Case for Affordable Housing"; Ashby, *Many Challenges Arise.*
26. Burkam, Lee, and Dwyer, "School Mobility in the Early Elementary Grades."
27. Mueller and Tighe, "Making the Case for Affordable Housing."

achievement, including standardized tests.[28] The biggest impact is on Black and low-income students.[29]

The most severe form of housing instability is homelessness. Homeless children have a unique set of concerns that could diminish their educational success, including transportation problems that affect attendance. Self-confidence suffers from the stigma and shame of homelessness as well as pessimism teachers may convey about the prospects of these students. Crowded and noisy conditions in shelters can also affect students' ability to complete assignments.[30]

Housing Affordability

Nearly half of renting households were "cost-burdened," paying more than 30 percent of their incomes for housing in 2016. One-quarter of renting households paid more than half of their income for housing. This leaves little money for other necessities. Among households in the lowest income quartile, income net of rent fell from $730 in 2001 to $590 in 2016, after adjusting for inflation. Households with children had just $490 left for other expenditures, including food, transportation, and health care.[31] It is not surprising that children from the lowest-income families perform more poorly in school than those from families

28. Kerbow, Azcoitia, and Buell, "Student Mobility and Local School Improvement in Chicago."

29. Raudenbush, Jean, and Art, "Year-by-Year and Cumulative Impacts of Attending a High-Mobility Elementary School."

30. Masten et al., "Educational Risks for Children Experiencing Homelessness."

31. Joint Center for Housing Studies of Harvard University, *The State of the Nation's Housing, 2018.*

living closer to the poverty line, who perform worse than those who are more financially secure.[32]

Neighborhoods

In addition to the quality and affordability of the physical housing that children live in, the characteristics of their neighborhoods can potentially affect academic achievement. Neighborhoods help determine students' access to educational and non-educational resources, the schools they attend, their peers and social networks, social norms and expectations, and their exposure to crime and violence. These factors, in addition to other neighborhood characteristics, may affect students' academic achievement and behavior in school.[33]

The social norms fostered by the environments in which children grow up influence students' own expectations. For example, if many students in their neighborhoods drop out of high school, participate in street organizations or illegal activities, or have teenage pregnancies, students may see these behaviors as the normal or most attractive options. Being around people who complete high school on time and go on to postsecondary education can raise the expectations young people have for themselves.[34]

There is not a consensus about how much neighborhoods, separately from other life circumstances, affect educational outcomes. It is difficult to disentangle the multiple environmental factors since families self-select into neighborhoods. Household income, access to support systems, personal motivation, and

---

32. Lacour and Tissington, "The Effects of Poverty on Academic Achievement."
33. Galster et al., "The Influence of Neighborhood Poverty during Childhood."
34. Ibid.

other factors clearly affect both where families live and how their kids do in school. However, several experimental studies have allowed researchers to strengthen their analyses and numerous nonexperimental studies also provide powerful evidence about the likely impact on children of growing up in impoverished and dangerous neighborhoods. The role of neighborhoods in determining children's futures has become more important as the number of children growing up in areas dominated by poverty has increased over time.

Concentration of Poverty

After declining between 1990 and 2000, the concentration of poverty in the United States has been increasing. Larger shares of low-income youth, especially Black and Hispanic youth, live in neighborhoods where more than 40 percent of the residents are poor. In 2016, one-quarter of the Black poor and 17 percent of the Hispanic poor lived in a neighborhood of extreme poverty, compared with 8 percent of the White poor. The share of preschool age children living in high-poverty neighborhoods is higher than the share of any other age group (table 4.1). The shares of all groups—including White children and adults— living in high-poverty areas have been increasing since before the Great Recession.[35]

A large body of nonexperimental research supports the idea that children who live in poor neighborhoods have weaker school outcomes than similar children living in less-disadvantaged neighborhoods.[36] The general consensus of research examining

35. Jargowsky, *The Architecture of Segregation.*

36. Harding, "Counterfactual Models of Neighborhood Effects"; Burdick-Will et al., "Converging Evidence for Neighborhood Effects on Children's Test Scores."

TABLE 4.1. Percentage of Population Living in High-Poverty Neighborhoods Nationwide, 2016

Evidence on the Effects of Neighborhood on Schooling Outcomes

		Age				
		0–5	6–11	12–17	Adults	All Ages
Total	Poor	16.5%	15.6%	14.7%	13.8%	14.4%
	Non-poor	2.7%	2.4%	2.5%	2.8%	2.7%
White	Poor	6.2%	5.2%	4.6%	8.2%	7.5%
	Non-poor	9.0%	0.7%	0.7%	1.2%	1.2%
Black	Poor	28.0%	26.6%	25.2%	24.2%	25.2%
	Non-poor	7.9%	7.6%	0.1%	9.3%	0.1%
Hispanic	Poor	18.1%	17.9%	17.6%	16.9%	17.4%
	Non-poor	5.3%	5.0%	5.0%	5.9%	5.7%

Source: Jargowsky, *The Architecture of Segregation*.
Note: High-poverty areas are defined as census tracts where 40 percent or more of the population is below the poverty level.

census tracts indicates that living in neighborhoods with concentrated poverty is detrimental to children's cognitive and academic development. Some of the harm comes from the physical characteristics of communities. For example, exposure to air pollution makes it more likely that children with respiratory problems will be absent from school. Students whose homes, schools, or classrooms are located under airline flight paths, near noisy highways, or adjacent to elevated train lines have lower reading skills than comparable students in quieter settings.[37]

A study of low-income households offered housing by the Denver Housing Authority determined that neighborhood unemployment and other indicators of financial instability were associated with higher rates of grade retention. Moreover, among those who enrolled in college, young people were more

37. Sharkey and Faber, "Where, When, Why, and for Whom Do Residential Contexts Matter?"; Marcotte, "Something in the Air?"

likely to drop out if they had moved to neighborhoods with high levels of property crime and less likely to drop out if they had moved to neighborhoods where adults had relatively high levels of occupational prestige. The effects were particularly large for Hispanic youth.[38] A study of a program giving housing vouchers to low-income families found that children moving to predominantly White suburbs were significantly less likely to drop out of school, were more often in college-track courses, and were more likely than others to enroll in four-year colleges.[39]

Differences in Schools or Differences in Neighborhoods?

Some studies, however, suggest that it is differences in schools—not the differences in neighborhoods themselves— that most affect student achievement. Students living in the same neighborhood but attending schools with different concentrations of low-income students have significantly different outcomes.[40] But researchers who find neighborhoods very important do not argue that schools and families are not also important. Rather, they contend that even good schools cannot fully compensate for the cognitive and emotional challenges of living in very problematic neighborhoods, at least at levels of expenditures per student in the current range. There is evidence that better schooling can improve achievement levels even for children who have grown up in highly adverse conditions but

38. Galster et al., "Neighborhood Effects on Secondary School Performance of Latino and African American Youth."

39. Rosenbaum, "Changing the Geography of Opportunity by Expanding Residential Choice."

40. Schwartz, *Housing Policy Is School Policy*.

not eliminate the gaps across children from dramatically different backgrounds.

In 1994, the United States Departments of Education and
Housing and Urban Development began a randomized experiment in Boston, Chicago, Los Angeles, and New York. The Moving to Opportunity (MTO) program offered housing vouchers
for low-income families to move from high-poverty neighborhoods to low-poverty neighborhoods. Families and students,
including both those who received vouchers and members of a
control group who had not received them, were surveyed four
to seven years later and again ten to fifteen years later.

Early analyses of the MTO results yielded mixed conclusions. Some found that moving from a high-poverty to a low-
poverty area did improve academic performance.[41] However, a
comprehensive study of the early results did not find statistically significant impacts on test scores four to seven years after
students relocated.[42]

A careful 2011 review of all available evidence reconciled these
findings, concluding that while neighborhoods do not always
have a significant impact on educational outcomes, living in severely economically distressed or dangerous environments such
as those found in Chicago and Baltimore does significantly reduce children's chances of succeeding.[43]

Recent findings from MTO have been clearer about the impact of neighborhoods on educational outcomes. Long-term
results show that moving to a better neighborhood before age

41. Leventhal and Brooks-Gunn, "A Randomized Study of Neighborhood
Effects."

42. Sanbonmatsu et al., "Neighborhoods and Academic Achievement"; Sanbonmatsu et al., *Moving to Opportunity for Fair Housing.*

43. Burdick-Will et al., "Converging Evidence for Neighborhood Effects on
Children's Test Scores."

thirteen significantly increased the probability of going to college, going to a more selective college, and graduating from college. But moving had a negative impact on outcomes for young people who moved when they were older, which the authors posit may be due to disruption and stressors related to moving.[44] Similarly, the amount of time children spend living in high-poverty neighborhoods is negatively correlated with high school completion.[45]

Some of the inconsistent findings about the extent to which neighborhoods—as opposed to the characteristics of the people living in those neighborhoods—affect residents' cognitive capacities and academic outcomes may result from the variation in effects across locations and populations. For example, the amount of time children reside in high-poverty neighborhoods, how connected they are to their communities, whether they go to local schools, whether they spend time elsewhere with family, and how old they are could strengthen or weaken the impact of the neighborhood on their development.[46]

The MTO experiment generated different outcomes in different cities. Researchers have hypothesized that the extent of deprivation in the communities from which the students moved could make a difference. Exposure to concentrated disadvantage over the course of childhood reduces the probability

44. Chetty, Hendren, and Katz, "The Effects of Exposure to Better Neighborhoods on Children."

45. Crowder and South, "Spatial and Temporal Dimensions of Neighborhood Effects"; Wodtke, Harding, and Elwert, "Neighborhood Effects in Temporal Perspective"; Chetty and Hendren, "The Impacts of Neighborhoods."

46. Sharkey and Faber, "Where, When, Why, and for Whom Do Residential Contexts Matter?"; Crowder and South, "Spatial and Temporal Dimensions of Neighborhood Effects"; Wodtke, Harding, and Elwert, "Neighborhood Effects in Temporal Perspective"; Chetty and Hendren, "The Impacts of Neighborhoods."

of high school graduation for all young people but appears to have a particularly large impact on Black students. Persistent disadvantage across generations appears to increase the damage children suffer from neighborhood problems.[47] This reality is particularly damaging to the chances of Black children, since more than half of Black families have lived in the poorest quarter of American neighborhoods over consecutive generations, compared to less than 10 percent of White families.[48]

It is possible that difficulties in controlling statistically for family income, parents' mental health, schools attended, and other factors lead to underestimation of the impact of neighborhoods, because these factors are partially the product of the neighborhoods in which parents have lived over their lifetimes. There is strong evidence that the influence of the residential environment persists and accumulates, affecting families over long periods of time.[49]

It is not easy to quantify the portion of school achievement gaps across socioeconomic and racial/ethnic groups that is directly attributable to housing quality and neighborhood characteristics. Many children who grow up in substandard housing and neighborhoods where crime and poverty are pervasive also live in families facing a range of difficulties, including physical and mental health problems, and attend poorly resourced schools with high concentrations of poverty. But there is little doubt that the poor living environments exacerbate the barriers these children face. Their circumstances make it much more

47. Wodtke, Harding, and Elwert, "Neighborhood Effects in Temporal Perspective."

48. Sharkey, "The Intergenerational Transmission of Context."

49. Wodtke, Harding, and Elwert, "Neighborhood Effects in Temporal Perspective."

difficult to learn and to develop the self-images, expectations, and self-confidence that would prepare them to enroll and succeed in college.

Health and Health Care Access

Students' health and access to health care can affect their attendance, ability to complete assignments, and behavior in school. Unfortunately, there are dramatic disparities in health and health care access along socioeconomic and racial lines. Despite increases in health insurance coverage since the implementation of the Affordable Care Act, 18 percent of individuals under the age of 65 living in households with incomes below the poverty level lacked health insurance in 2017—still a substantial decline from 28–30 percent between 2005 and 2012. In contrast, only 7 percent of those with incomes above 200 percent of the poverty level lacked coverage—a decline from 9–11 percent between 2005 and 2012.[50]

The literature around student health points to several mechanisms through which health affects students' capacity to learn and their educational outcomes: sensory perceptions or the ability to see and hear clearly; cognition; school connectedness and engagement; absenteeism; and temporary or permanent dropping out.[51]

Researchers have looked at how health as early as in utero can affect long-term educational outcomes. For example, twins with higher birth weights are more likely to enter school with higher test scores and this trend persists throughout elementary

50. Cohen, Zammitti, and Martinez, *Health Insurance Coverage.*
51. Basch, "Healthier Students Are Better Learners."

school and beyond.[52] Students with low birth weights are less likely than others to graduate from high school.[53]

Access to health care during childhood and the associated effects on health improve elementary and middle school reading scores[54] and appear to have a measurable impact on post-secondary attainment. A study of the expansion of Medicaid coverage for children found a significant decline in the high school dropout rate and a 2.3 to 3.0 percent increase in bachelor's degree completion.[55]

Inadequate nutrition is an obvious mechanism through which poverty can affect health and the ability to participate fully in school. There is considerable evidence that food insecurity interferes with children's health and development. Not having enough to eat is associated with lower math scores, grade repetition, and a range of other behavioral and psychological issues interfering with elementary school performance.[56]

Lack of adequate dental care also has a clear impact on children's ability to learn. From 2011 to 2014, 19 percent of children ages 5 to 19 had untreated dental problems, with the frequency ranging from 15 percent of Asian and 17 percent of White children to 23 percent of Black children and 24 percent of those of Mexican origin. Only 9 percent of those from families with incomes of four times the poverty level or higher, but

52. Figlio et al., "The Effects of Poor Neonatal Health on Children's Cognitive Development."

53. Oreopoulos et al., "The Short-, Medium-, and Long-Term Consequences of Poor Infant Health"; Conley and Bennett, "Is Biology Destiny?"

54. Levine and Schanzenbach, "The Impact of Children's Public Health Insurance Expansions."

55. Cohodes et al., "The Effect of Child Health Insurance Access on Schooling."

56. Jyoti, Frongillo, and Jones, "Food Insecurity Affects School Children's Academic Performance, Weight Gain, and Social Skills."

one-quarter of children from families below the poverty level, had untreated dental problems.[57] Students suffering from toothaches are more likely than others to have low GPAs. Those without access to dental care have high rates of absenteeism.[58]

Early Childhood Education

Researchers, using evidence from Head Start, the Abecedarian Project, and Perry Preschool, have found evidence that interventions as early as prekindergarten can affect long-term educational outcomes, supporting the concept of dynamic complementarity. However, children whose parents do not have four-year college degrees are less likely than others to be in preschool programs (table 4.2).

Head Start is primarily an early childhood education program for low-income children. In existence since 1965, this program has provided the basis for numerous studies attempting to measure the effects of early childhood education. Much of the research on the long-term effects of the program finds that Head Start's academic benefits—as measured by test scores—may fade by the time participants reach third grade. Yet not all the benefits of Head Start must be channeled through higher test scores: social-emotional learning is an important aspect of early education. At least one rigorous study found a positive impact on high school completion rates and college enrollment,[59] and another found a positive effect on high school graduation rates and college attendance for White Head Start participants and a

57. National Center for Health Statistics, *Untreated Dental Caries.*

58. Seirawan, Faust, and Mulligan, "The Impact of Oral Health on the Academic Performance of Disadvantaged Children."

59. Ludwig and Miller, "Does Head Start Improve Children's Life Chances?"

TABLE 4.2. Share of 3- to 5-Year-Olds Enrolled in
Preschool or Kindergarten, 2018

The share of children enrolled in preschool or
kindergarten increases with parents' level of education.

Total	64%
Parents' highest education	
Less than HS	58%
HS/GED	57%
Some college/no degree	59%
Associate degree	64%
Bachelor's degree	68%
Graduate or professional degree	73%

Source: U.S. Department of Education, Digest of Education
Statistics, 2019, table 202.20.

significant decrease in arrests for Black participants.[60] David
Deming used a study design based on comparing long-term outcomes for siblings who were exposed to Head Start in differing
degrees and found significant long-run effects of the program.[61]
Studies of other preschool programs have also found significant
positive effects on high school graduation and college enrollment rates.[62]

Because of the important effects that exposure to high-
quality prekindergarten can have on children and particularly
low-income children, socioeconomic and racial disparities in
access and exposure have implications for inequality. Investments in early childhood education could improve school
readiness among disadvantaged children. Improving school
readiness will be an important step in mitigating the effects of
inequalities present in later education for disadvantaged

60. Garces, Thomas, and Currie, "Long Term Effects of Head Start."
61. Deming, "Early Childhood Intervention and Life-Cycle Skill Development."
62. Carolina Abecedarian Project, "Scholarly Publications."

students. Starting investments in proven programs early on and continually investing during early childhood could play a large role in mitigating inequality. The principle of dynamic complementarity implies that these early investments will also make later schooling investments more productive, while reductions in support for elementary education will undercut the value of earlier investments.

K–12 Experiences

Having had such a wide range of experience in the early years of their lives, children from different backgrounds enter school with very different levels of academic readiness. For example, on math tests where the average score was 36.1, the scores of children entering kindergarten in 2010 ranged from 31.4 for Hispanic children and 32.0 for Black children to 38.7 for White children and 40.5 for Asian children. Those whose parents had not completed high school averaged 27.7, compared with 35.0 for those whose parents had some college experience but not a bachelor's degree and 43.2 for those whose parents had earned a graduate or professional degree. The average score was 30.5 for children living below the poverty level and 39.9 for those whose families had incomes of 200 percent of the poverty level or higher (table 4.3).

Early childhood experiences that lead to gaps in school readiness follow children through their school years. Children who have lived in poverty are much more likely than others to leave school without a high school diploma, and those who have spent more time in poverty are most vulnerable.[63] As the gaps in test scores across children from different socioeconomic

63. Hernandez, *Double Jeopardy*.

TABLE 4.3. Fall 2010 First-Time Kindergartners' Mathematics Scale Scores through Spring of Fifth Grade

Large differences in mathematical achievement by socioeconomic status emerge by the time children enter kindergarten.

	Mean Mathematics Score for Children Entering Kindergarten, 2010	Mean Mathematics Score in 5th Grade, Spring 2016	5th grade Score/ Kindergarten Score
Total	36.1	120.0	3.3
Race/Ethnicity			
White	38.7	124.7	3.2
Black	32.0	108.6	3.4
Hispanic	31.4	114.2	3.6
Asian	40.5	127.8	3.2
Parents' highest education level			
Less than high school	27.7	108.4	3.9
High school completion	31.2	113.2	3.6
Some college/vocational	35.0	118.5	3.4
Bachelor's degree	39.9	125.9	3.2
Any graduate education	43.2	129.5	3.0
Poverty status			
Below poverty threshold	30.5	111.3	3.6
100 to 199% of poverty level	34.5	118.3	3.4
200% or more of poverty level	39.9	125.6	3.1

Source: U.S. Department of Education, *Digest of Education Statistics, 2019*, table 220.41.

backgrounds have grown, the gaps in the amount of schooling they complete have also grown.[64] Socioeconomic differences in children's skills in reading and math, their ability to pay attention, and their level of antisocial behavior persist or grow over the school years, contributing to—but not fully explaining—later

64. Duncan and Murnane, "Introduction."

TABLE 4.4. Shares of Students Attending Low- and High-Poverty-Rate Schools, 2017–18

Black and Hispanic students are more likely than others to attend schools with high concentrations of poverty.

	Share of Students in School Districts with Poverty Rate 10% or Lower, 2017–18	Share of Students in School Districts with Poverty Rate over 23%, 2017–18
Total	25%	26%
White	35%	15%
Black	10%	46%
Hispanic	13%	36%
Asian	41%	18%

Source: U.S. Department of Education, *Digest of Education Statistics, 2019*, table 203.75.

outcomes, including postsecondary attainment and labor market earnings.[65]

Despite some progress in narrowing gaps in school funding levels, schools have become more segregated by income over time. In 2017–18, one-quarter of children attended schools where 10 percent or less of the students lived in households with incomes below the poverty level; one-quarter attended schools where the poverty rate was over 23 percent. However, 46 percent of Black children and 36 percent of Hispanic children were enrolled in these high-poverty schools, compared with just 15 percent of White children (table 4.4).

The decline in racial segregation generated by judicial enforcement of civil rights legislation has been reversed. For example, the share of Black children attending schools where less than a quarter of the students are nonwhite fell from 11 percent

---

65. Duncan and Magnuson, "The Nature and Impact of Early Achievement Skills."

TABLE 4.5. Racial Segregation at Public Schools over Time

The share of Black students attending schools that enroll very few White students has increased over time.

Year	Share of Black Students Attending Schools That Are Less than 25% Nonwhite	Share of Black Students Attending Schools That Are More than 75% Nonwhite	Share of Hispanic Students Attending Schools That Are Less than 25% Nonwhite	Share of Hispanic Students Attending Schools That Are More than 75% Nonwhite	Share of White Students Attending Schools That Are More than 75% White
1995	11%	47%	10%	53%	72%
2000	9%	51%	9%	56%	69%
2005	9%	52%	8%	58%	65%
2010	7%	55%	6%	59%	57%
2015	5%	58%	6%	60%	51%
2016	5%	58%	6%	60%	50%
2017	4%	58%	5%	60%	48%

Source: U.S. Department of Education, *Digest of Education Statistics, 2019*, table 216.50.

in 1995 to 9 percent in 2005 and 4 percent in 2017. The share of Black children attending schools that were more than 75 percent nonwhite rose from 47 percent to 52 percent to 58 percent over these years. The pattern for Hispanic students is similar. Because the share of students who are White is declining over time, White students are, however, less and less likely to attend schools where more than three-quarters of the students are White (table 4.5).

Even with the obstacles low-income students face prior to starting school, attending different schools would increase the probability of low-income students going to college. One study indicated that moving a student from a school in the 10th percentile in terms of quality to a 90th percentile school would increase the probability of graduating from high school by 8 to

10 percentage points and the probability of going to a four-year college by about 20 percentage points.[66]

Children's test scores are significantly affected by other students in the classroom. Recent evidence indicates that going to elementary school with children who have been exposed to domestic violence has long-term negative impacts, reducing high school test scores, college degree attainment, and adult earnings.[67] Children from low socioeconomic and minority backgrounds are more likely than others to experience disruptive behavior, gang activity, and crime at school. For example, in 2017–18, at 16 percent of the public schools where three-quarters or more of the students were eligible for free or reduced-price lunches, student acts of disrespect for teachers other than verbal abuse happened at least once a week. This was the pattern at only 6 percent of the schools where less than one-quarter of the students qualified for this program for low-income families. Gang activities were an issue at 17 percent of the schools with the largest shares of low-income students but at only 3 percent of those with the smallest shares. The frequency of crime and violent crime in the schools followed similar patterns (table 4.6).

Narrowing the gaps in K–12 experiences among students from different family backgrounds is a vital but very challenging task. The issues are closely connected to all of the other inequalities this chapter discusses. Money is not the only answer, but increased funding for elementary and secondary education, targeting disadvantaged and underserved students in

66. Altonji and Mansfield, "The Role of Family, Community, and School Characteristics."

67. Carrell, Hoekstra, and Kuka, "The Long-Run Effects of Disruptive Peers."

TABLE 4.6. Variation in Disruptive Activity at Public Schools, 2017–18

Crime and other disruptive activities are much more prevalent at high-poverty schools than at schools enrolling more affluent student bodies.

Share of Eligible for Free or Reduced-Price Lunch	Percentage of Public Schools Where Student Acts of Disrespect for Teachers Other than Verbal Abuse Happen at Least Once a Week	Percentage of Public Schools Where Gang Activities Occur	Crime Incidents Reported per 1,000 Students	Violent Crime Incidents Reported per 1,000 Students
0 to 25%	6%	3%	14%	7%
26% to 50%	8%	8%	25%	15%
51% to 75%	14%	12%	33%	22%
76% to 100%	16%	17%	40%	30%

Source: U.S. Department of Education, Digest of Education Statistics, 2019, tables 230.10, 229.20.

both urban and rural areas, is almost certainly part of the solution.

The United States spends more per student on elementary and secondary education than most developed countries do. In 2017, the $14,100 per full-time-equivalent student in the United States compared with highs of $21,900 in Luxembourg and $15,600 in Austria and Norway, but with $12,800 in Sweden, $11,900 in Canada, and lower numbers in most other countries.[68]

However, the United States spends less on pre-college education relative to postsecondary education than most other wealthy countries do—41 cents for each dollar on higher education (figure 4.1). Much of the spending on higher education in this country is private—from tuition payments, endowments, and other private sources. But shifting the balance could improve

68. National Center for Education Statistics, "Education Expenditures by Country," https://nces.ed.gov/programs/coe/indicator/cmd.

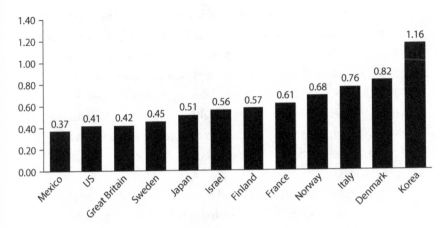

FIGURE 4.1. Spending on Pre-college Education as a Share of Spending on Post-secondary Education, 2016
The United States devotes less of its education spending to the pre-college years than other nations do.

Source: OECD, *Data: Education Spending.*

opportunities for students from low SES backgrounds at all levels of education.

Policy Solutions

Increased funding for broad-access postsecondary institutions, more generous need-based grant aid, a stronger safety net for students struggling to meet basic needs, and a concerted effort to implement evidence-based policies that increase college success for at-risk students are all important components of the effort to reduce inequality in educational attainment. Ameliorating the stratification of students into different types of institutions based on socioeconomic background has the potential to increase completion rates and promote upward mobility.

Such improvements are vitally important, but the reality is that these measures alone can never be enough in a society as riven by inequality as ours has become. As we have discussed in detail in this chapter, young people have dramatically different life experiences in the years leading up to the door of college. Policies to improve the neighborhoods and housing in which children grow up and to increase access to quality health care and early childhood, elementary, and secondary education are critical.

Despite the fact that elementary and secondary school are largely mandatory and free, gaps in high school graduation rates and in the academic achievement levels of students who do manage to graduate are dramatic. Our nation urgently needs redoubled efforts at the postsecondary levels of education to overcome some of the consequences for students who grow up in a society that seems all but indifferent to their human dignity and prospects. But even extreme efforts will not be enough to eliminate the differences in preparation to enroll and succeed in college associated with socioeconomic background without a concerted effort to reduce economic inequality and to nurture, support, and educate children whose parents struggle to meet their needs.

As we look ahead to future generations, the most fundamental thing we as a nation can do is to see to it that young people are not born into such dramatically unequal circumstances as they are now. This requires policy changes and institutional improvements in all of our major social institutions. It involves everything from the taxation of income and wealth to labor market policies, protection of voting rights, and of course education at all levels, in addition to the focus on housing, nutrition, health care, and early childhood highlighted in this chapter. The more we can accomplish through policy improvements and

institutional reform throughout the life cycle, the less overwhelming the burden of trying to compensate for the effects on
children of growing up in adverse circumstances will be.

It is beyond the scope of this book to make judgments about
the relative merits of rental assistance and policies that support
homeownership or between policies that focus on increasing
the supply of affordable housing and those that provide vouchers to help households pay. Similarly, we will not enter the debate about the most effective way to reduce racial segregation
in the schools. Experts in these fields—as well as in community
development, access to health care, and other critical areas—
have amassed significant evidence about what works.

There will always be differences in priorities, differences in
opinion about which studies are most reliable, and conflicting
judgments about issues including funding, the roles of different
levels of government, and the role of race and discrimination in
creating barriers for families and children. But these circumstances should not stand in the way of building a consensus that
improving the lives of children and making it possible for those
from all backgrounds to grow up prepared to take advantage of
educational opportunities should be very high on the public
agenda. Without real progress in these efforts, changes at the
college level will be limited in the extent to which they can solve
the inequality problems highlighted in this book.

In the end, though, the vast differences in starting points between children born to privilege and those born to deprivation
in a society as vastly unequal as ours has become will not be
fully overcome by even the most ingenious and well-funded
government programs targeted at disadvantaged children. It is
only when the starting points themselves become more nearly
equal that real equality of opportunity will come into view.

The Message of the Pandemic

Families of all backgrounds and resource levels have struggled in the face of COVID-19. But more affluent families have been much better situated to manage their way through difficulties and to meet the developmental and educational needs of their young children. Well-off parents with white-collar jobs are more likely to be able to work at home and provide care for their children when they can't go to school than are others.[69] They have been able, for example, to afford to place their children in "learning pods" where children can be schooled relatively safely. For those who are kept home, better-off parents can provide a better-equipped and quieter space for living and learning.

Moreover, new research indicates that students from disadvantaged backgrounds are more likely to be required to learn remotely, a practice that has been shown to be generally less effective than in-person learning. One indicator of the disparity is that closed schools during the pandemic were about 25 percent less White in their racial composition than schools that remained open.[70]

Many parents had to venture into the world to work throughout the COVID crisis because their jobs simply cannot be performed at a distance. But many were compelled to leave home regardless of their health because businesses and governments resisted making it too "comfortable" for them to stay safe and keep their kids safe at home by providing for sick leave, generous unemployment compensation, and rent relief—all factors

69. British Broadcasting Company, "What Remote Jobs Tell Us about Inequality."

70. Parolin and Lee, "Large Socio-Economic, Geographic, and Demographic Disparities Exist."

that might help them if they did not report for work.[71] We can have some confidence that restaurants, retail stores, and even movie theaters will recover from the pandemic, but we fear that the setbacks to young children's learning will be far harder to recover from.

Summary

Young people from affluent families are more likely to go to college than those from less privileged backgrounds. When they enroll in college, they are more likely than others to attend four-year public and private nonprofit institutions, more likely to complete their programs, and more likely to earn bachelor's degrees, as opposed to associate degrees or short-term certificates. All of these gaps raise questions about the extent to which higher education facilitates upward mobility and reduces inequality across people from different socioeconomic backgrounds.

But regardless of how much more selective colleges and universities might do to enroll and support low-income and first-generation students, and how much further states could go in ensuring adequate funding for the institutions serving the majority of low- and moderate-income students, it is clear that students reach college age in vastly unequal circumstances. The families, neighborhoods, housing, schools, health care—and an array of other environmental factors—with which they have grown up have left some ready to take advantage of all the opportunities with which they might be presented—and others with such limited academic and social skills and such low expectations that the idea of continuing their education may seem

71. According to former Vice President Mike Pence, "[Democrats] ... want to make rich people poor and make poor people more comfortable" (Pence, Turning Point USA).

unrealistic. The occasional story of a young person who has risen from extremely deprived circumstances to reach academic and professional heights can provide valuable inspiration (and well-deserved admiration) but should not blind us to the reality that it is precisely because these stories are so rare that they gain so much attention.

Distinguishing the separate influences of differences in financial resources; parental time, knowledge, and stress; housing quality; neighborhood characteristics; access to medical and dental care; high-quality preschool; and elementary and secondary schooling is challenging. But it is clear that all of these factors work together to create gaps in the developed capacity of children from different backgrounds to learn and to achieve in school. The gaps are already large when children start kindergarten and they do not narrow by the time they graduate from—or fail to graduate from—high school. Early experiences become integral parts of individuals' neurological and psychological makeup.[72] Changes in brain function contribute to the reality that learning begets learning. The barriers that colleges and universities must help students from disadvantaged backgrounds overcome are not just financial and academic. They are the deeply rooted effects of challenging childhood circumstances.

A central question is the extent to which education— elementary and secondary education and/or higher education— can compensate for the environmental differences that lead to large gaps in readiness to learn when children reach kindergarten and, later, in cognitive and non-cognitive skills across young people when they reach college age. By this time, differences in the quality of K–12 schooling have likely reinforced the early childhood differences. The potential answers to these questions

72. Nelson and Sheridan, "Lessons from Neuroscience Research."

carry very different policy implications. The most optimistic view is that while limited resources and bad neighborhoods have negative effects on students' lives, effective schooling can reliably and fully overcome these bad effects, no matter how serious. This is one interpretation of the "no excuses" view of schooling's role.[73] At the other extreme is the argument that the negative effects of bad environments are so decisive that there is "no point" in investing in schooling until the living conditions of poor students have been substantially ameliorated.[74] It is not clear that anyone holds these views in absolute terms, and the debate usually takes place in the context of elementary/secondary education. But the "no excuses" versus "no point" perspectives help to frame thinking about postsecondary education as well. Should we expect colleges and universities to erase the differences among the students who come to their doors? Should we resign ourselves to a significant share of young people being simply unable to accomplish college-level work?

As should be clear, our views fall between the extremes: almost regardless of young people's backgrounds, better education will improve their lives. But until we get serious about substantially reducing the inequalities in the lives of children, we should anticipate only limited success in making college success more equal.

73. Thernstrom and Thernstrom, *No Excuses.*
74. Ladd, "Education and Poverty."

CHAPTER 5
After College

Earlier chapters focused on educational attainment across adults from different socioeconomic backgrounds and the reality that the circumstances in which children grow up contribute to these gaps. We now ask how differences in the quantity and type of college education people experience affect their chances of finding a satisfying career path that allows them to support themselves and their families at a reasonable standard of living.

The dramatic inequality of incomes and wealth in the United States exacerbates the differences between the opportunities available to those who earn valuable college degrees and those who do not achieve this outcome. Economic inequality in the United States has grown over time and far exceeds the inequality in many other developed countries. This inequality is both cause and effect of the relatively large gaps in earnings among people with different levels of education in the United States. These gaps make the earnings penalty for not completing a college education higher in this country than in most of the rest of the world.

These large inequalities in people's post-schooling economic status also play a major role in shaping the educational and social opportunities of their children and thus in passing the inequalities forward into the next generation. As we observed in chapter 2, income is simply a useful proxy for the many things that really matter, like having time to spend with your children and the resources to see to their health and their personal development, as well as to participate politically to promote and defend your own and your children's interests. The size of the gaps in market earnings and the differences in life experiences associated with those inequalities—and hence the prospects of the next generation—are influenced not only by the supply and demand for skills but also by the distribution of market power, laws that regulate businesses and protect workers, and other factors. Moreover, progressive tax and transfer policies can mute the effects of gaps in market earnings between more and less educated workers. We examine the extent to which this occurs in the United States in comparison to other countries.

The Labor Market

Changes over time in earnings inequality and the forces contributing to that inequality shed light on the relationships among the distribution of educational attainment, the return to postsecondary degrees, and economic inequality.

Growing Inequality

Income inequality has increased over time. One measure of inequality is the share of personal income accruing to families at different levels of the income distribution. If income were equally distributed, 20 percent of families would receive 20 percent of the income. But the share of income going to the highest-income fifth of families rose from 41 percent in 1969 to 47 percent in 1999

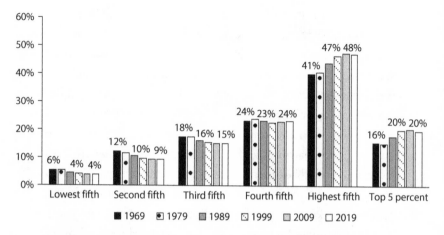

FIGURE 5.1. Share of Aggregate Income Received by Each Fifth and Top 5 Percent of Families, 1969–2019
Over the past fifty years, average incomes have increased for the most affluent families but declined for others.

Source: U.S. Census Bureau, *Current Population Survey*, Annual Social and Economic Supplement, 2020, table F-2.

and 48 percent in 2019. The share of income accruing to the top 5 percent of families increased from 16 percent to 20 percent over these fifty years. The share going to the lowest-income 20 percent of families fell from 5.6 percent in 1969 to 4.3 percent in 1999 to 3.8 percent in 2019. The second and third quintiles have also received lower shares of total income over time (figure 5.1).

The College Earnings Premium Is at an All-Time High

As documented in detail by Claudia Goldin and Lawrence Katz in their groundbreaking book, *The Race between Education and Technology*, changes in the supply of and demand for highly skilled workers explain much of the rise in the earnings premium for a college education over the 1980–2010 period. And the increase in the education wage premium explains more than half of the rise in inequality in those decades, which is reflected primarily in growing gaps between those at the top of the income distribution and those in the middle, rather than between those in the middle and those at the bottom.[1] Since 2010, the earnings premium has stopped rising but has remained at its historically high level.

The increase in wage inequality in the United States has made the level of education individuals complete more important in determining how they will fare economically. And much of that increase in inequality has taken the form of more rapid wage growth among workers with more education. The driving force in the growing wage gap in favor of more educated workers was a slowdown in the relative growth in the supply of highly educated workers. In the period before 1980, growth in the demand for high-skilled workers had been matched by steady growth in the supply of such workers. But from 1980 to 2005, slower growth on the supply side caused the wage premium to rise even though the rate of growth in demand for high-skilled labor was actually lower than the growth in demand for less-skilled labor. Meanwhile the decline in the value of the minimum wage and in the role of unions also put downward pressure on the wages of less educated workers.[2]

---

1. Goldin and Katz, "Long-Run Changes in the Wage Structure"; Lemieux, "Postsecondary Education and Increasing Wage Inequality"; Autor, Katz, and Kearney, "The Polarization of the US Labor Market."

2. Goldin and Katz, *The Race between Education and Technology*; Autor, Manning, and Smith, "The Contribution of the Minimum Wage to U.S. Wage Inequality over Three Decades."

As David Autor argues, "The rising skill premium is not, of course, the sole cause of growing inequality. The decades-long decline in the real value of the U.S. minimum wage, the sharp drops in non-college employment opportunities in production, clerical, and administrative support positions stemming from automation, the steep rise in international competition from the developing world, the secularly declining membership and bargaining power of U.S. labor unions, and the successive enactment of multiple reductions in top federal marginal tax rates have all served to magnify inequality and erode real wages among less educated workers."[3]

That said, according to Autor, absent the slowdown in growth in the supply of college graduates after 1980, the long-term increase in the skill premium in the U.S. labor market might well not have occurred. Indeed, between 2004 and 2012, the supply of workers with bachelor's degrees again grew relatively rapidly—and the growth in the college wage premium stagnated (while remaining quite high by historical standards).[4]

Increasing the share of adults with college degrees—and particularly with high-quality bachelor's degrees—would be a constructive path to reducing inequality in the labor market because this group would command smaller wage premiums if there were more of them relative to the number of jobs requiring their skills. Workers would become more productive because of their higher levels of education, and the changes in the relative supplies of more-skilled and less-skilled workers would reduce the earnings gap between these groups.

3. Autor, "Skills, Education, and the Rise of Earnings Inequality."
4. Ibid.

Who Would Benefit from Expanding College Completion?

The impact of increasing educational attainment on both in-equality and economic mobility depends in part on how post-secondary education affects people who start out in different situations. It might be tempting to think that inducing more people to go to college or to stay in college to complete their programs is a questionable strategy because the new students may be less well-prepared or motivated than those who now enroll in and complete college. It is reasonable to expect that students who have been most successful in high school might benefit most from going to college. The admissions process, which selects students with the strongest academic records, is compatible with this idea. We invest most in the college educa-tion of those who have already proven themselves—particularly if they are able to pay.

But there is powerful evidence suggesting that there is more to the story than this. Some people weigh the costs and benefits and decide not to go to college. They understand the potential earnings premium and could finance their education—possibly by borrowing. But others lack the information and/or the re-sources and don't see college as an option. Pushing those in the former group to enroll might not yield much benefit for them or for society, because they are, for whatever reason, making a reasoned choice. Removing barriers preventing the latter group from enrolling is likely to be a more productive option.[5]

Some studies indicate that the incremental benefits associ-ated with college education are higher for those with weaker beginnings. Other evidence suggests that it is those in the middle

5. Card, "Estimating the Return to Schooling."

who benefit most from college: Those at the top tend to do well regardless of their college experiences and those at the bottom struggle regardless of their paths, but for those in the middle, education makes the difference.[6]

Institutional factors in the broader economy, which may be more amenable than the supply of and demand for college-educated workers to shorter-term policy fixes, also contribute to earnings inequality. Some researchers have emphasized increasing managerial power and the weakening of unions as forces increasing the dispersion of earnings. The unusually large gap between the share of income going to the top 20 percent of the population and the bottom 20 percent in the United States, documented below, reflects international differences in social and institutional structures. Social norms against outsized earnings also appear to have weakened in the United States. Strategies that strengthen unions, increase the minimum wage, and expand the social safety net would diminish the current chasm in living standards between those near the upper end of the income distribution and others.[7]

Is the Return to a College Education Too High or Too Low?

The rising price of college has increased concern over the size of the return to a college education. The return on this investment depends on both the earnings premium—the earnings differential between those with and without college degrees—and the price of education. With a given earnings premium, the return on the investment declines as students pay more and spend more time completing their degrees.

6. Attewell and Lavin, *Passing the Torch*; Brand and Xie, "Who Benefits Most from College?"
7. Berg, "Labour Market Institutions."

The discussion of inequality in the labor market suggests that, in fact, a reduction in inequality can come about through a smaller earnings premium for college degrees. Yet as the investment required to earn a college degree increases, the earnings premium has to be larger to maintain a high rate of return. Naysayers have increasingly contended that it may no longer be worthwhile in economic terms for young people to go to college (advice they rarely seem to direct toward their own children). In fact, the earnings premium for a bachelor's degree is about as high as it has ever been. And the average return— not only to bachelor's degrees but also to associate degrees, which have a considerably lower earnings premium (but are also typically substantially less costly for students) and for which there is a great deal of variation in the extent to which they pay off in the labor market—remains high enough to justify the investment.

The earnings gap is the easiest indicator of the benefits of college to measure. And increases in this gap explain a significant amount of the increase over time in income inequality in the United States. The greater the difference in earnings between typical high school graduates and typical college graduates, the greater the gaps between those in the lower and upper halves of the income distribution. The earnings premium for a college education has to be high enough to make it worth the investment for students, but that does not mean it has to keep growing indefinitely or even to remain higher than needed to justify the investment.

The laws of supply and demand imply that if more people had college degrees—if the supply of workers with college degrees was higher—there would be downward pressure on earnings for this group. This happened in the 1960s and early 1970s, when the share of people attending college right after high school rose quickly from a low base. The change was rapid enough to outpace the demand for workers with college backgrounds, which put downward pressure on college wages. Indeed, low wages and high unemployment among college-educated workers led Richard Freeman to write *The Overeducated American* in 1976. But this excess supply of higher-skilled workers was short-lived. By 1980, growth in the educational attainment of new generations of workers had begun to slow, and the lasting rise in the wage premium began.

Were we to achieve a sustained increase in college attainment that outpaced growing demand for high-skill workers, this change would leave fewer people with only a high school education—increasing demand relative to supply for this group and possibly putting upward pressure on the wage levels of the less educated. These tendencies could be reinforced by policy actions like raising the minimum wage or making the tax system more progressive.

As noted earlier, averages conceal considerable variation in earnings among adults with similar levels of education. A number of factors contribute to these differences, including differences in skills and motivation, occupations, and discrimination based on gender and race. But differences in the colleges and universities students attend also matter.

It Matters Where You Go to College

Inequality by Race and Ethnicity within Levels of Education

Earnings inequality among those with the same level of education is also an important issue. Earning a bachelor's degree significantly increases the earnings prospects for members of all demographic groups. But Black and Hispanic four-year college

TABLE 5.1. Median Earnings of Four-Year College Graduates Ages 35 to 44, by Race and Ethnicity, 2019

Black and Hispanic adults earn less than Asian and White adults of the same age with the same level of education.

Race/Ethnicity	BA or higher	BA	Relative to All BA or higher	BA
All	$78,700	$70,900	1.00	1.00
White	$79,100	$72,000	1.01	1.02
Asian	$96,200	$78,900	1.22	1.11
Black	$65,600	$57,300	0.83	0.81
Hispanic	$69,700	$61,900	0.89	0.87

Source: U.S. Census Bureau, *Current Population Survey,* Annual Social and Economic Supplement, 2020, table PINC-03.
Note: Includes only full-time year-round workers.

graduates typically have lower earnings than others; White and Asian graduates do better than the overall average.[8]

In 2019, median earnings for adults ages 35 to 44 whose highest degree was a bachelor's degree and who worked full time year-round ranged from $57,300 for Black workers to $78,900 for Asian workers. Including those who have earned advanced degrees after they completed their bachelor's degrees yields similar differences, with the median for Asians 22 percent higher than the overall median and the median for Black 35- to 44-year-old full-time workers just 83 percent of the overall median (table 5.1).

Even within racial/ethnic groups of adults ages 35–44 who are working full time year-round there is considerable variation in earnings. The share earning less than $50,000 in 2019 ranged from 21 percent of Asians whose highest degree was a

8. Blacks who did not attend college likewise earn less than their White counterparts, so the economic return to college is similar to that for Whites despite lower college wages.

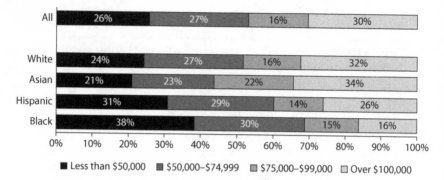

FIGURE 5.2. Distribution of Earnings of Adults Ages 35 to 44 with Bachelor's Degrees Working Full Time Year-Round by Race and Ethnicity, 2019
Black and Hispanic adults with bachelor's degrees earn less than White and Asian adults with the same level of education.

Source: U.S. Census Bureau, *Current Population Survey,* Annual Social and Economic Supplement, 2020, table PINC-03.

bachelor's degree to 38 percent of Black workers with the same level of education. The share earning $100,000 or more ranged from 16 percent of Black bachelor's degree holders to 34 percent of Asians (figure 5.2).

Inequality Associated with College Characteristics

The sorting of undergraduate students from different socioeconomic backgrounds into colleges with different levels of resources and selectivity documented in chapter 3 might not be too much of a problem if the chances of completing a degree were similar across institutions and if post-college earnings and other outcomes were similar regardless of where students earn their degrees.

There is, however, strong evidence that this is not the case. Similar students have a significantly higher chance of earning a bachelor's degree if they begin college at a four-year institution instead of a two-year institution—and if they enroll in the most selective institution at which they can be accepted. Moreover, as discussed in chapter 3, despite some inconsistency in the findings, there is broad consensus that graduates of higher-selectivity colleges and universities earn more and have other more positive life outcomes than similar students who attend lower-selectivity institutions.

Highly selective colleges and universities and the increasing competition for acceptance at these institutions receive an enormous amount of attention. The recent scandal involving very wealthy parents paying others to alter their children's test scores or take the tests for them, as well as to create counterfeit athletic careers for them, is an extreme example. But the focus on these institutions has sharpened as highly qualified—and affluent—students from all over the country have gravitated to this small sliver of higher education. Caroline Hoxby's research indicates that the increasing concentration of high-ability students at a small number of colleges and universities is associated with growing gaps in the resources devoted to educating students at different types of institutions. Investments in students are increasingly correlated with their measured academic abilities, as the resource gaps across institutions grow and well-prepared students are increasingly concentrated in a small number of selective institutions.[9]

Per-student spending on instruction at institutions that accept 25 percent of their applicants or less is three and a half times as high as spending at institutions that accept at least half of their applicants. That difference is greater within the private nonprofit sector than among public institutions. It's not only high spending levels at the elite institutions that create this

9. Hoxby, "The Changing Selectivity of American Colleges."

TABLE 5.2. Instructional Spending per Student by Institutional Selectivity, 2017–18

Spending per student is higher at more selective institutions.

	Instructional Expenditures per Full-Time-Equivalent Student		
	Public	Private nonprofit	All
Less selective (accept 50% or more)	$8,800	$7,600	$8,200
Moderately selective (accept 25% to 50%)	$11,300	$12,500	$11,800
Very selective (accept 25% or less)	$20,500	$31,500	$28,900
Very selective/less selective	2.3	4.1	3.5
Very selective/moderately selective	1.8	2.5	2.5
Moderately selective/less selective	1.3	1.6	1.4

Source: U.S. Department of Education, Integrated Postsecondary Education Data System. Calculations by the authors.
Note: Estimates for all institutions include for-profit as well as public and private nonprofit institutions. Graduate students are weighted as equivalent to three undergraduate students because of typical differences in spending levels.

difference. Spending differences between moderately selective and less selective institutions are also sizable (table 5.2).

The students at these wealthy, highly selective colleges and universities receive large subsidies, as even the high tuition prices they face cover a relatively small share of the cost of their education. In contrast, students at less selective institutions pay a larger share of the smaller cost of their education. In 2016–17, 46 percent of the $46,000 per student spent at private nonprofit research universities came in the form of subsidy from non-tuition revenues. In contrast, only 15 percent of the $19,000 per student spent at private nonprofit master's degree universities was above and beyond students' tuition payments.[10] While there is variation among institutions in both of these categories,

10. Ma et al., Trends in College Pricing, 2019.

both endowment wealth and selectivity are much higher at research universities.

Spending on students is also skewed toward students at more selective institutions in the public sector. In 2017–18, public doctoral universities spent about 40 percent more per student than public master's institutions and about 80 percent more than public two-year colleges.[11]

COMPLETION RATES

It is unsurprising that institutions that enroll students with the strongest academic credentials have the highest completion rates, but the gaps are startling. The share of students beginning at four-year institutions in 2011 who completed a bachelor's degree at their first institution within six years ranged from 31 percent at open admissions institutions to 62 percent at those accepting 50 to 75 percent of applicants—and 87 percent at those accepting less than 25 percent of their applicants.[12]

It is, of course, not easy to define or measure college quality. Researchers use some combination of variables including the average SAT/ACT scores of students, the shares of applicants accepted, faculty/student ratios, and educational expenditures per student to differentiate postsecondary institutions by quality. Differences in bachelor's degree completion rates for similar students who attend institutions of different quality have been documented by a number of researchers. The problem they observe, with students from low-income backgrounds particularly likely to attend less selective institutions than those they could

11. Ibid.
12. U.S. Department of Education, *Digest of Education Statistics, 2018*, table 326.10.

qualify for, and graduation rates correlated with quality, has been dubbed the "undermatch" problem. It is important to underscore that the undermatch analysis goes beyond the unsurprising observation that schools with high admissions standards have high graduation rates. The further claim is that the *same* student has a higher likelihood of graduating from college if she attends a more rather than a less selective place.

The problem is not just that we do not create enough of the kinds of learning environments in which students who do not have stellar academic preparation can thrive. The undermatch problem is that students with strong qualifications lower their chances of graduating by attending less-selective institutions.[13] Some qualified low-income applicants are rejected from selective institutions because of their financial need, but many low-income students and those from underrepresented racial and ethnic groups do not apply to the selective institutions that would admit them.

EARNINGS

As discussed in chapter 3, even for students who graduate, where they earned their degrees matters. It is reasonable to believe that if there were less earnings dispersion in the labor market, there would be smaller income gaps among adults with similar levels of education, and sorting of students into postsecondary institutions would matter less—at least among those who graduate.

13. Bowen, Chingos, and McPherson, "Helping Students Finish the 4-Year Run"; Roderick et al., *From High School to the Future.*

International Comparisons

Greater inequality in the labor market—a larger gap between the earnings of more- and less-skilled workers—makes life harder for those without a postsecondary education. The problem is particularly acute in the United States, where inequality is higher than in most developed countries.

An intuitively appealing benchmark is the ratio of the pay of CEOs to that of the average worker. In 2014, when the ratio was 48:1 in Denmark, 84:1 in the United Kingdom, and 147:1 in Germany, it was 354:1 in the United States.[14]

The Gini coefficient is a common measure of inequality, ranging from 0 in a country where everyone has the same income to 1 in a country where one person has all of the income. The Gini is directly related to a measure of how far apart the average difference in incomes is between any two people picked at random.[15]

In 2018, the Gini coefficient was .390 in the United States, compared to an average of .316 for the 36 countries that are members of the Organisation for Economic Cooperation and Development (OECD). Values ranged from .236 for the Slovak Republic, with the lowest level of inequality, and .262 for Norway to .289 for Germany, .301 for France, and .339 for Japan. Very few countries tracked by the OECD have more inequality than the United States, according to this measure (figure 5.3).

A similar perspective comes from comparing the ratio of the average income of the top 20 percent of households to the average income of the bottom 20 percent of households. In 2018 that

14. Statista, "Ratio between CEOs and Average Workers in World in 2014."

15. The average difference expressed as a fraction of mean income is twice the Gini. See Taylor, "What Is a Gini Coefficient?"

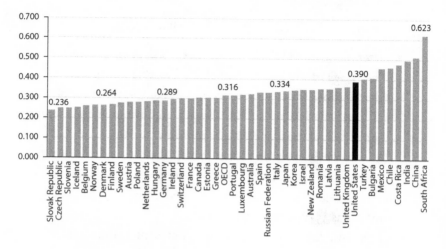

FIGURE 5.3. Inequality across Nations: Gini Coefficients, 2018
Income inequality is higher in the United States than in other Western countries.

Source: OECD, "Key Indicators on the Distribution of Household Disposable Income and Poverty, 2007, 2016 and 2017 or Most Recent Year."

ratio was 8.4 in the United States. In contrast, the top 20 percent in France had 4.6 times the income of the bottom 20 percent and the average across OECD countries was 5.4 (figure 5.4).

The countries that have high levels of inequality also have large earnings differentials between adults with bachelor's degrees or higher and those with only a secondary education. Data on the earnings gaps are not available for all of the countries, but Chile and Costa Rica, where inequality is higher than in the United States, also have the largest earnings premiums for postsecondary degrees.

According to OECD data, median earnings for bachelor's degree recipients in the United States are 70 percent higher than those for high school graduates. The average for the EU is 38 percent and in Denmark the gap is just 10 percent. The gap

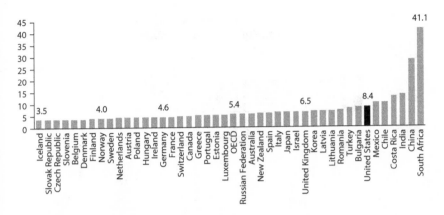

FIGURE 5.4. Inequality across Nations: Average Income of Highest 20 Percent of Households Relative to Income of Lowest 20 Percent of Households, 2018
The income gap between those at the top and those at the bottom is larger in the United States than in most other countries.

Source: OECD, "Key Indicators on the Distribution of Household Disposable Income and Poverty, 2007, 2016 and 2017 or Most Recent Year."

between bachelor's degrees and advanced degrees is also large in the United States (figure 5.5).

The gap between those with bachelor's degrees and those with shorter-term postsecondary credentials is also relatively large in the United States—49 percent compared with 10 percent across the European Union. Short-term postsecondary credentials pay off better in many Western European and Scandinavian countries than in the United States.

The combination of these patterns sheds light on the relationship between the earnings premium for postsecondary education and income inequality. The gap between the earnings of adults with a bachelor's degree or higher and those with lower levels of educational attainment is larger in the United States than in other developed countries. This pattern is reflected in higher overall levels of income inequality. Data are

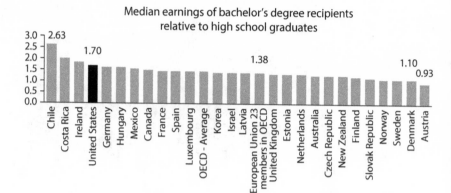

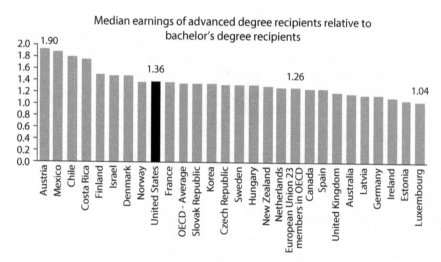

FIGURE 5.5. Median Earnings Ratios by Level of Education: International Comparisons

The earnings premium for a bachelor's degree is larger in the United States than in most other countries, but the payoff to short-term postsecondary degrees is smaller.

Source: OECD, "Education and Earnings."

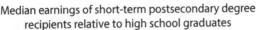

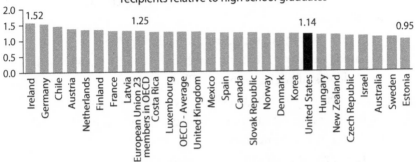

Median earnings of short-term postsecondary degree recipients relative to high school graduates

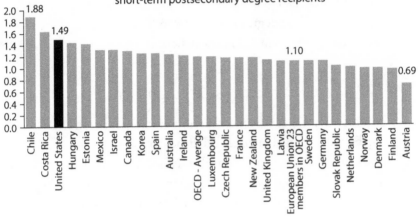

Median earnings of bachelor's degree recipients relative to short-term postsecondary degree recipients

FIGURE 5.5. (*Continued*)

available for twenty-eight countries on both the Gini coefficient and the gap in earnings between bachelor's degree recipients and high school graduates. The nine countries (including the United States) with the largest earnings premiums (ranging from 55 percent to 163 percent) have the highest inequality measures with an average Gini coefficient of .366. The nine countries with the smallest earnings premiums (ranging from 12 percent to 34 percent) have the lowest inequality indexes—averaging .286. And the average Gini coefficient for the countries in the middle is .324.

Higher earnings premiums for bachelor's degrees are associated not only with higher levels of inequality but also with lower levels of social mobility. Children of better-educated parents tend to attain higher levels of education—and as a result higher earnings—than those who grew up in less-educated households, where incomes are lower.[16]

The correlation between socioeconomic background and educational attainment has more serious implications in the United States than in many other nations because not earning a four-year college degree has more significant implications for lifetime earnings than it does elsewhere.

Market Income vs. Disposable Income

Another factor that influences lifetime earnings is the size of the gap between market income and disposable income. So far, this chapter has focused on households' market incomes—the amount of earnings they receive prior to either the taxes they pay or any government transfers (such as Social Security retirement benefits). Disposable income refers instead to income after allowing for taxes and transfers. Taxes and transfers can make for quite a large difference between what people are paid in the marketplace and the income they have to spend at the grocery store, save for a vacation, or pay debts. Usually we would expect that higher-income people pay a larger fraction of their income in taxes than lower-income people do and that transfer payments go disproportionately to lower-income

16. Autor, "Skills, Education, and the Rise of Earnings Inequality."

people. When this is so, disposable income will be more equal than market income.

On the tax side, while the U.S. federal government relies heavily on a relatively progressive income tax system to raise revenue, the Social Security system is financed through a regressive payroll tax. Overall tax progressivity is also limited in the United States by very generous protections for income from capital gains and by the effective absence of taxation on inheritances. Moreover, state and local taxes are on balance regressive, leading two prominent economists to conclude recently that the United States effectively has a flat tax system, taking roughly the same proportion of income from the better-off as from the less well-off.[17] The Affordable Care Act, both through subsidizing health insurance and through its tax-based financing system, has increased the progressivity of the overall system. A more progressive system, and one with fewer exemptions that favor the well-off, could help raise the revenues needed to finance a more generous and effective system of transfers to the needy.

The largest component of government transfer payments is the old-age pension program of Social Security. While an essential element of the safety net, this program has relatively little redistributive impact and is targeted on elderly people rather than on children and the young. A major aim of this book is to identify ways to use government transfers to help ensure that children have a strong start in life, improving their chances to later become successful college students. It is therefore particularly disappointing to learn that the United States is notably less successful than its Anglophone counterparts (Great Britain, Ireland, Australia, and Canada) in keeping the rate of child poverty—especially of deep poverty—low.

17. Saez and Zucman, *The Triumph of Injustice.*

A good way to describe the impact of taxes and transfers on inequality in the rich countries is to compare market income inequality to disposable income inequality in countries with similar market inequalities. Austria, Belgium, France, Finland, Germany, the United Kingdom, and the United States all have similar market (pre-tax and transfer) inequality as measured by the Gini coefficient discussed earlier in this chapter. The Gini is between .50 and .52 in all of these countries. But the first five countries use taxes and transfers to reduce this measure of inequality to between .27 and .29, a decrease of 42 to 48 percent. The United States, on the other hand, decreases the Gini to .39, a decline of less than 25 percent (figure 5.6). (In the UK, taxes and transfers reduce the Gini from .51 to .36.)

Twenty percent of American children live in families with incomes below half of the U.S. median income, compared with 9 percent in Ireland, 11 percent in Great Britain, 13 percent in Australia, and 16 percent in Canada below their countries' medians, according to the National Academies recent report, *A Roadmap to Reducing Child Poverty*.[18] Even more concerning are the facts about deep poverty, measured as a low absolute standard of disposable income. For the Anglophone countries named above, the deep poverty rate for families with children ranges from 1.1 percent in Canada to 1.9 percent in Australia; for the United States it is 3.6 percent, nearly double that of the next worst performer.[19] Children in the deep poverty group face a host of serious problems. Their generally poor health status, increased likelihood of exposure to lead in their homes, and a

---

18. National Academies of Sciences, Engineering, and Medicine, *A Roadmap to Reducing Child Poverty*, 140.

19. Ibid., 62. Dates range by country between 2010 and 2014. For detail on deep poverty, see pp. 386ff.

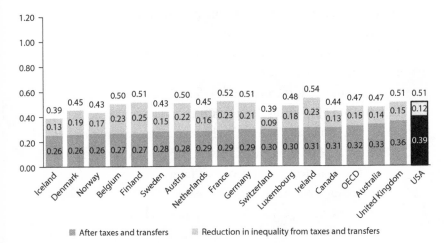

FIGURE 5.6. Inequality before and after Taxes and Transfers, 2016
The tax and transfer system does less to reduce income inequality in the United States than in other high-income countries.

Note: The selection of relatively high-income countries for comparison is based on estimates of GDP/cap at data.oecd.org/gdp/gross-domestic-product-gdp.htm. The figures are for 2016 or most recent available date.
Source: OECD, *Government at a Glance, 2019,* figure 10.7.

range of other issues contribute to lower standardized test scores and other conditions worsening their chances for success in education and work.

A major factor in explaining the greater prevalence of deep poverty in the United States is that most transfer payments to help families in this country are employment related. The tie between employment and family benefits is notably visible with the large Earned Income Tax Credit (EITC). Even the Child Tax Credit is more generous for those who are employed. The effect, if not always the intent, of tying programs that support children in poverty to parents' workplace success is to make children's opportunities to develop successfully depend on factors for which the children are obviously not responsible.

An extreme example of the problem with these policies is that they exacerbate the serious consequences of mass incarceration, which removes so many parents (especially African Americans) from the labor force.

The National Academies study referenced above offers a set of reforms and innovations in government policy aimed at cutting child poverty in half. The report gives prominent attention to expanding the EITC substantially but also to providing more transfer programs aimed at supporting children in poverty regardless of the employment status of their parents. These reforms include making the existing Child Tax Credit fully refundable, introducing a new income-tested child allowance program, and using government funds to ensure that all single parents receive at least a minimal level of child support. The Covid-19 relief bill signed into law in March 2021 takes significant steps in the proposed direction, making the EITC more generous and expanding and restructuring the Child Tax Credit—for one year. Some estimates suggested that these changes could cut the child poverty rate from 14 percent to 7 percent.[20] The question is whether these new measures will become permanent and signal a new direction for U.S. policy.

Policy Directions

Over the long run, making progress toward a society of greater equality and fairness requires examining unequal chances not only among children or college students but also among adults in their post-college lives.

Narrowing the gaps in educational attainment across people from different backgrounds has the potential to diminish

20. Pulliam and Reeves, "New Child Tax Credit."

significantly the association between accidents of birth and adult outcomes. But as long as the dramatic inequality that characterizes the current U.S. labor market and economy persists it will be difficult even to check the growth in, let alone to diminish, the gaps in well-being across households. Reducing such gaps is important for building more equal starting points for the next generation. Moreover, if there were less distance between the earnings of adults with four-year college degrees and those with lower levels of education, people would have a more varied menu of choices about which educational and career paths best fit their talents and ambitions.

Public policies to reduce inequality can operate either by reducing gaps in market incomes or by using taxes and transfers to reduce the gaps in disposable incomes generated by the market.[21] Public policies influence market inequalities in earnings both through regulations that protect workers directly and through policies that reduce the market power of businesses.

Labor Market Policies

Since the early twentieth century, working conditions and wages in the United States have been regulated by both federal and state governments. Wages and hours laws, rights to collective

---

21. Some analysts draw a contrast between "predistribution"—modifying the income inequalities markets generate—and "redistribution"—government intervention to "correct" or modify the distribution the market generates. See Hacker, "The Institutional Foundations of Middle-Class Democracy." However, O'Neill ("Power, Predistribution, and Social Justice") points out that in an economy that evolves through time this distinction is less clear-cut than it might seem. So, for example, using taxes to finance larger welfare payments to families with small children might be classed as redistribution, but if it results in better education for low-income students and hence higher incomes in the next generation, that looks like predistribution.

bargaining and union representation, health and safety protections, unemployment compensation, and other regulations support workers' bargaining power and protect them from exploitation.

Minimum wage policies are particularly visible. The federal minimum wage has been frozen at $7.25 an hour since 2009, but it is higher in many states. California, the District of Columbia, Florida, Illinois, Maryland, Massachusetts, and New Jersey have all passed legislation to increase the minimum wage to $15 an hour over the next few years.[22] The debate about how high the minimum wage should be, how rapidly to increase it, and particularly whether it should be the same everywhere regardless of prevailing wages and cost of living is active and nuanced. For many decades, economists cautioned that high minimum wages might substantially reduce employment. However, in the last twenty years, improved empirical methods have provided strong evidence that the trade-offs (if any) are more favorable than previously thought, at least over some range. There is little doubt that allowing the minimum wage to decline in real terms over time has harmed workers struggling to make ends meet, and the National Academies of Sciences consensus report on reducing child poverty in the United States cited above recommended an increase in the federal minimum wage as an effective poverty-fighting strategy.[23]

Raising the minimum wage will not in itself solve the problems of the working poor. It will affect only a limited subset of workers, with the size of that group depending on how large the increase is. However, putting a higher floor under earnings may

22. National Conference of State Legislatures, "State Minimum Wages."

23. National Academies of Sciences, Engineering, and Medicine, *A Roadmap to Reducing Child Poverty*, 140.

have indirect effects, as by inducing employers to increase wages for higher-income workers to preserve their relative standing in the workplace.

The decline of unions is another factor contributing to increasing wage inequality. The share of workers belonging to a union in the United States fell from 20.1 percent in 1983 to 10.5 percent in 2018. Only 6.4 percent of private sector workers now belong to unions.[24] Although only 8 percent of French workers are unionized, unions are more prevalent in most other developed countries than in the United States. For example, more than 60 percent of workers in Denmark, Finland, and Sweden belong to unions, as do 34 percent in Italy, 28 percent in Canada and Israel, and 24 percent in the United Kingdom.[25]

Corporate Regulation and Anti-Trust Enforcement

Workers' incomes and opportunities are powerfully influenced by the concerted efforts of business owners, including the shareholders of corporations, to gain bargaining advantage at the expense of their rivals, their customers, and their workers. While economists often celebrate the advantages for the economy of widespread competition, investors and business strategists often emphasize the advantages individual companies gain through exerting market power. The celebrated investor Warren Buffett reports that he looks for companies "with durable competitive advantage"—"castles with moats."[26] Economists increasingly emphasize the capacity of leading firms in technology, finance, and other industries to use devices including lobbying, patent

---

24. U.S. Department of Labor, "Union Members Summary."
25. International Labor Organization, "Industrial Relations," 4.
26. Rasmussen, "The Gospel According to Michael Porter."

protection, and mergers to accumulate market power that can be used to increase profitability and reduce labor's share of earnings.[27] There is also a strong case that corporate investment in defending monopoly positions discourages innovation, wastes resources, and weakens political democracy.

Stricter enforcement of anti-trust laws could increase the market wages of workers in the lower ranges of the income distribution. In particular, the market power of employers who dominate industries and limit the opportunities of workers to change jobs holds wages down. Non-compete clauses for low-wage workers provide a clear example. It is not surprising that the Coca-Cola company would make great efforts to block its executives from moving straight to Pepsi. But about 15 percent of low-wage workers without college degrees are subject to such agreements. For example, before agreeing to drop the clause as part of a settlement with the state of New York, Jimmy John's required its workers to sign away the right to work at any sandwich shop within three miles of any franchise in the chain for up to two years after leaving the company. Bartenders, manicurists, and others in similar occupations are subject to similar restrictions.[28] Banning this practice would increase the bargaining power and job opportunities of low-wage workers while also making markets more efficient.

The pandemic that began in 2020 offered some stark examples of corporate power being used to erode worker protections, from lobbying for immunity from lawsuits over inadequate arrangements for social distancing to opposing extensions of

27. Stansbury and Summers, "Declining Worker Power and American Economic Performance."

28. Cornish, "Study Finds Many Companies Require Non-Compete Clauses for Low-Wage Workers."

supplemental unemployment compensation to pressure workers back into worksites.

Tax and Transfer Policies

Taxes and transfers should not be seen only as part of a separate "fiscal policy" system. They have important implications for child development and for human capital development generally. Strengthening support for children is especially important for combating deep poverty, which for all the reasons reviewed in chapter 4 can be devastating for children's success in school and in later life. As we write in early 2021, both Republicans and Democrats are showing increased interest in proposals to address child poverty through the transfer system.[29] Strong policies of this sort could have a significant impact on inequality in postsecondary opportunities and outcomes.

Conclusion

The failures of the American educational and social systems from birth on have fed economic inequality by restricting the number of Americans who succeed in earning college degrees. This effect has been compounded by a U.S. labor market with a low national minimum wage, weak labor unions, and regulatory policies that, especially recently, have strongly favored business over labor interests. The impact of these inequality-promoting tendencies has been further compounded by the presence in the United States of one of the least progressive tax and transfer systems in the developed world, which does less to

29. Romney, *Family Security Act*; Stein, "Senior Democrats Drafting Plan to Give Parents at Least $3,000 per Child in Biden Stimulus."

reduce inequality in disposable income than these policies in most developed countries do. It is hardly a surprise given all this that we are caught in a spiral of inequality where each new generation starts off life in more unequal circumstances than the preceding generation.

The question of what our nation can do to check and then reverse this spiral is one of great moment for our future. In what follows we examine the ways in which policies and practices in higher education—at both the individual institution level and the governmental level—can play a constructive role in addressing this historic challenge. We also explain why some persistently popular policy ideas for higher education reform, including "free tuition" and widespread loan forgiveness, would likely be counterproductive in the circumstances of the United States.

CHAPTER 6

What Can Colleges and Universities Do?

Our principal focus in this chapter is on actions higher education institutions could undertake that have the potential to reduce inequality of educational opportunities and outcomes, both in their own student bodies and more widely, as well as to address income inequality and limited social mobility more broadly. In the next chapter, we will examine the public policies adopted by state and federal governments that provide the framework within which American institutions of higher education operate and which influence the funding streams that support them. Within these constraints, institutions themselves are afforded considerable freedom over their own priorities and operations.

Addressing the successes and failures of higher education in increasing opportunities for economic and social mobility and in reducing inequality requires a clear view of people's lives before and after college. Both colleges and universities themselves and the public policies that shape, support, and constrain them can and should move in constructive directions. But only if the environments in which children grow up and the opportunities that they face become more equal will all young people be prepared to make the most of the postsecondary experience. And only if the labor market and surrounding social institutions do a better job of supporting people with different skills and capacities will higher education make real inroads into narrowing the gaps in living standards in our nation.

Arresting and then reversing our nation's slide toward ever greater inequality of income, wealth, and opportunity requires society-wide investments and reforms. These include investments in health, housing, and other areas of social welfare policy. They also involve reform of the tax system and of economic regulation, as we have discussed in earlier chapters. And, quite prominently, they require ambitious investment in education, beginning at the earliest ages and continuing throughout people's lives. A serious and sustained attack on growing social and economic inequality requires a society-wide mobilization with both policy experts and people of influence in all these arenas paying consistent attention to institutional reforms and policy actions that can reduce inequality.

It is important that higher education institutions and policymakers play their part in this effort by redoubling their own efforts to move our colleges and universities to do more to combat rising inequality and distribute opportunities more equitably.

The United States has never had a unified "system" of higher education in the way that some nations in Europe do. Every state operates public colleges and universities of its own. In addition, almost two thousand private nonprofit colleges and universities enroll students from throughout this country and the world. And as of 2018–19, there were 742 degree-granting for-profit postsecondary institutions (a decline from 1,451 in fall 2012).[1]

These thousands of higher education institutions vary enormously in size, mission, and history. In most cases, while the presidents and governing boards have considerable discretion over how they operate, they are all subject to the fundamental constraint that they need to raise enough money from a combination of governments, families, and philanthropic giving to pay the bills. As we show below, this basic financial constraint makes it a real challenge even for well-intentioned institutions to do as much as we might wish they would to combat inequality and promote social mobility. Financial constraints affect the more highly selective colleges and universities, which educate a relatively small share of the nation's undergraduate students and a still smaller share of those from low- and moderate-income families, differently from the broad-access institutions that are responsible for educating most students, particularly those seeking to move up the ladder.

University presidents and other on-campus leaders are also constrained by both legal and structural restrictions on their spending, as well as the sharing of power, formally and informally, with a range of interest groups and constituencies, including faculty, trustees, student groups, alumni, donors, and groups in the local community. These realities present obstacles to universities' efforts to direct available resources to where they may be most needed and best used.

We begin with a discussion of selective colleges and universities. Only 22 percent of first-year undergraduate students are enrolled at institutions that accept less than half of their applicants. Just 5 percent attend institutions that accept less than

1. U.S. Department of Education, *Digest of Education Statistics, 2019*, table 317.10.

one-quarter of their applicants.[2] These highly selective places garner a disproportionate share of the attention of news and magazine editors, at least in part because many of them graduated from these colleges and they want their children to attend them. But, despite the attention the elites garner, improving outcomes at the less selective colleges and universities—including community colleges, most of which will admit any student with a high school degree or the equivalent—has far more potential for producing large-scale change in the lives and economic prospects of the majority of Americans, especially those from low- and moderate-income families, than anything we can do at the most selective colleges and universities.

What Real Difference Can Elite Institutions Make?

Nonetheless, there is significant room for high-selectivity institutions to lessen inequality and promote greater opportunity and social mobility. Moreover, these elite institutions have the opportunity to influence society through avenues other than deciding whom to enroll, including how they educate their students toward their social responsibilities and how they can help their communities.

Recruit, Enroll, and Support More Students from Low- and Moderate-Income Backgrounds

Much of the attention to the issue of inequality in higher education has focused on the role of the small number of well-resourced institutions with highly selective admissions. On one

2. U.S. Department of Education, *Digest of Education Statistics, 2018*, table 305.40.

hand, critics claim that it doesn't really matter whether students attend these colleges or not and that paying those high tuitions is a waste.[3] On the other hand, there is considerable frustration with the small share of students at these elite institutions who come from low- and moderate-income households. As discussed in depth in chapter 3, there is convincing evidence that the quality of the institutions *does* matter for student outcomes and it is worth asking what these more selective colleges and universities can do both to further diversify the socioeconomic backgrounds of their student bodies and, more broadly, to contribute to social mobility and the reduction of inequality in society.

There is a real question whether the extreme selectivity at the handful of private universities and colleges at the pinnacle serves any meaningful academic, social, or economic purpose beyond providing an outlet for the energies of students (and parents) seeking status. We have our doubts. We have in the past made the case that the very wealthiest and most selective colleges and universities should expand their enrollment, easing the competitive pressure a bit and spreading their wealth across a larger, if still tiny, number of students.[4] But these most extreme cases are not at the core of the nation's inequality issues.

Once we go beyond these possibly irrational extremes, sorting students according to their developed abilities and dispositions to do the hard work of learning at a demanding college makes sense. The opportunities available at elite institutions are certainly a function of the resources at their disposal. But they are also in large part a function of their student bodies.

---

3. See, for example, Ip, "Is Elite College Worth It?"; Hess and Fuller, "The Pay-off for a Prestigious College."
4. Baum and McPherson, "Sorting to Extremes."

Interacting with well-prepared, high-achieving, highly motivated peers is a significant component of the experience qualified low-income students who attend less selective institutions
miss out on. These peer relationships may also have lasting
value for students' personal lives and social and business connections. These provide a further reason for seeking diversity
in the composition of the student body at these institutions.

The solution, in our view, is *not* to do away with selective
admissions in the interest of increasing opportunity. Rather,
selective institutions, both public and private, should do a
much better job of identifying and recruiting from among the
substantial number of low-income students who could qualify
but do not even apply to these institutions. In 2015–16, about
300,000 undergraduate students from families with incomes
below $50,000 had scored 1250 or higher on the SAT (or had a
comparable score on the ACT). This is a very good score. Only
40 percent of these high-scoring, low-income students attended
very selective institutions—compared with almost 60 percent
of those from families with incomes of $200,000 or higher with
similar scores.[5] Recruiting these students does not require giving
up on selectivity.

Moreover, highly selective institutions could make further
progress simply by adjusting their standards to the same extent
that they do now for so-called legacy students, the children of
alumni. There is good evidence that modifying admissions criteria at selective institutions in this modest way has the potential to significantly increase the share of lower-income students
at these colleges and, thus, the number of their students experiencing upward mobility. (It is worth remembering that many
of these same institutions "bend" their admissions criteria a lot

5. U.S. Department of Education, *National Postsecondary Student Aid Study, 2016.*

further for student athletes than they do for either legacy admits or students of color.)[6] According to recent research from Raj Chetty and colleagues, granting admissions considerations to low- and middle-income students similar to those currently offered to legacy students at elite private colleges could largely eliminate differences in the way students with similar academic credentials from families with different incomes are distributed across these colleges.[7]

Further evidence about the impact of attending more selective institutions comes from a recent study of the outcomes of the Texas Top Ten Percent rule. Since 1998, students in the top 10 percent of their high school classes have been guaranteed admission to any Texas public university. More students at the top of their classes at high schools where few students have historically attended selective institutions—primarily schools with students from low-income backgrounds—now attend the University of Texas-Austin. The trade-off is that fewer students with similar levels of academic achievement attending high schools in more affluent neighborhoods with higher college-going rates have the opportunity to attend the flagship institution. The study found that college enrollment, bachelor's degree attainment, and future earnings were all higher for the students who benefited from the Top Ten Percent rule. Outcomes were no worse for the students they replaced, who attended less selective institutions but did not have lower enrollment rates, graduation rates, or earnings than they would otherwise have had.[8]

6. Shulman and Bowen, *The Game of Life.*

7. Chetty et al., "The Determinants of Income Segregation and Intergenerational Mobility." The proposal to put a "thumb on the scale" for low-income admission equivalent to that provided for legacies was advanced by Bowen, Kurzweil, and Tobin in *Equity and Excellence in American Higher Education.*

8. Black, Denning, and Rothstein, "Winners and Losers?"

This study—like the research cited in chapter 3—suggests that college quality/selectivity does not affect all students the same way. Apparently, students from backgrounds where college education is more widespread and social networks provide connections to economically successful people are less dependent on the benefits offered by more selective institutions. So, the benefits of opening the doors to lower SES students, even without increasing total enrollment in those colleges, significantly outweigh any costs to those not admitted.

The idea is not that standards should be compromised but that students from less privileged backgrounds should be given a boost similar to that given at many institutions to legacies and athletes. Moreover, a policy of providing an admissions preference to lower-income students is not vulnerable to a legal challenge based on the Fourteenth Amendment as race-based affirmative action has been. In our view, such "class-based" affirmative action is best seen as a complement rather than substitute for race-based affirmative action.

Yet once you move beyond the few best-funded institutions in both the private and public sectors, many of the rest lack the resources required to pay for the student aid that would allow a significantly larger number of talented low-income students to enroll and succeed. Some of these high-achieving low-income students are therefore turned down in favor of less well-qualified students who can pay. Some institutions choose instead to admit more of their qualified low-income applicants, but with an unreasonably high loan burden in their financial aid packages. Fewer than twenty-five private colleges and universities in the United States commit to admitting students without reference to their ability to pay and meeting their full demonstrated need for financial assistance.[9]

9. These institutions comprise the 568 group. See 568group.org.

TOUGH TRADE-OFFS CONFRONT
MOST INSTITUTIONS

Institutions face difficult trade-offs. Admitting more students from low-income families has to be paid for, perhaps by squeezing faculty salaries or increasing teaching loads, by refusing to support study abroad through the college's budget, or by raising class sizes. The catch-22 for colleges and universities that push too hard in these directions is that they may lose full-pay students to other places that don't make this trade-off, thus worsening the financial trap. In the competitive marketplace of U.S. higher education, the fundamental constraint of raising enough revenue to pay the bills can conflict with even the best intentions. Drawing down the endowment may help in the short run, but as the endowment shrinks, so does the ability to sustain institutional quality, and therefore make attendance so desirable.

Thus, for many selective institutions outside the wealthiest few, the big challenges to becoming more egalitarian in admissions are identifying and recruiting the promising low-income students who are out there and helping them pay for their education, problems that will not be solved by lowering admissions standards or putting a thumb on the scale for those from less privileged backgrounds.

A small number of very selective institutions hold a large share of all endowment assets and some of these could support more low-income students without jeopardizing the extraordinary quality of the opportunities they provide. But as Chetty and co-authors note, the recruitment challenge is greater at these few most selective institutions because of the relatively small number of low-income students meeting their admission requirements.

However, for those institutions just below this tier—say, those accepting 15 to 50 percent of their applicants—the pool is larger. This group would include flagship public universities in addition to almost half of private nonprofit institutions. Unfortunately, most of those institutions do not have the same very large endowments as the few wealthiest, most selective schools. Nonetheless, a combination of financial aid and pricing policies, spending priorities, and state incentives could lead to significant progress in breaking down the barriers for low- and moderate-income student access to private, and particularly public, selective colleges and universities. Despite the correlation between socioeconomic background and almost all criteria central to the selective admissions process, increasing SES diversity does not need to depend on compromising high intellectual and academic admissions standards.[10] It does, however, cost money.

Even private institutions do after all get significant support through tax breaks and federal student aid and should shoulder the responsibility to enroll more socioeconomically diverse student bodies—but ultimately, both their priorities and their financial constraints shape their decisions.

Educating Students to Value and Contribute to a More Equitable Society

Facilitating upward mobility for individual students is not the only important contribution colleges and universities make to reducing social inequities. Much debate about admissions policies is relevant only to selective institutions. As noted, a very small share of undergraduate students attends selective institutions. In fact, if highly selective institutions served only to advance the interests of the relatively small number of students they enroll, there would be very limited potential for them to make a difference commensurate with their resources.

10. Hoxby and Avery, "The Missing 'One-Offs.'"

The faculty at many universities generate research that has benefits extending far beyond the confines of campus. Other activities also have considerable external reach. But even in the circumscribed area of educating undergraduate students, academic institutions can affect the lives of many non-students and even the fundamental structures of society.

If most of the talented and well-educated graduates of these institutions lead lives dedicated only to their own personal and financial well-being, the positive impact will be small even if significantly more low-income students enroll. But if these institutions focus on creating an environment and a curriculum that foster deeper social awareness and preparation for citizenship, they will graduate more students whose lives focus on broader social concerns. As Harry Brighouse has argued, the best justification for the substantial investment society makes in the education of students at top universities may lie in the contributions they can make, directly and indirectly, to the future well-being of less privileged people.[11] We encourage colleges to develop and report metrics of their graduates' contributions that go beyond simply looking to see how many have high incomes. How many go into public service or work in philanthropy? How many have leadership positions in their communities?

Using Resources to Support Surrounding Communities and Students Who Will Enroll Elsewhere

The skewed distribution of resources across colleges and universities and the financial, social, and academic barriers facing many students make a compelling argument for well-resourced institutions to dedicate some of their funds to improving educational

11. Brighouse, "Ethical Leadership in Hard Times."

opportunities and outcomes for students whose life circumstances prevent them from attending selective colleges and universities. There are limits to the feasibility of this type of activity, since endowment funds, private giving, and state appropriations are, by and large, specifically provided for the purpose of supporting the institution and its students. But many institutions view supporting their communities as integral to their missions and expanding this role could contribute far more to increasing opportunities than enrolling a few more high-achieving low-income students.

For example, the University of Wisconsin-Eau Claire works with local public schools to improve college readiness and to encourage all students to see a college degree as a realistic possibility. The university provides tutors, runs after-school programs, and hosts special camps in robotics and coding. Colby College is actively engaged in the revitalization of downtown Waterville, Maine, working closely with community members, constructing a dormitory and a hotel, and bringing in investors.[12] The University of Virginia is developing affordable housing units on university-owned land. Stanford University and the University at Buffalo have similar goals.[13]

Individual institutions understandably focus on recruiting promising students of color or low-income students to their own institutions but in doing so may overlook the greater impact they can have by combining their efforts to reach a broader pool of students. With significant funding from Yale University, private colleges and universities in New Haven have joined together to fund and support the New Haven Promise, providing

12. Fischer, "Tackling the Equity Challenge from All Sides."
13. Whitford, "UVA Unveils Affordable Housing Project."

incentives, preparation, and resources for New Haven students attending college in Connecticut.[14]

Over one thousand colleges participate in Campus Compact, which helps institutions design programs to develop citizenship skills in their students and build community partnerships. The basic premise is that colleges and universities are "anchor institutions" that are interdependent with their communities.[15] Some institutions participate in business development, support for affordable housing or a mixed-use community, or address the digital divide in their communities.[16] Other institutions have committed to using a small share of their endowment funds to strengthen their communities.[17]

All of these efforts have the potential to improve the lives of young people, strengthening their prospects of completing high school and going on to college—possibly to selective colleges and universities and possibly to earn bachelor's degrees.

The accumulating evidence that college quality matters most for first-generation students and those from low-income households and that diminishing the stratification of students by family income across institutions has the potential to facilitate social mobility provides strong arguments for working toward solutions.

But elite institutions can do much more than just increase the socioeconomic diversity of their student bodies. They should focus on the mission of educating active citizens with community values and broadening their reach beyond the walls of their campuses.

14. New Haven Promise, "New Haven Promise."
15. Campus Compact, https://compact.org/.
16. Community-wealth.org.
17. Ibid.

How Can Broad-Access Institutions
Improve Outcomes for Their Students?

Selective colleges and universities, both public and private, do have a significant role to play in lessening the inequalities that plague our society. One of their roles is to find students from low-income and first-generation college families who can qualify for admission at selective places and recruit them more successfully.

But the fact is that, even if there were no limits on how much selective institutions could grow without compromising the quality of the education they offer, the majority of high school graduates simply are not prepared for success at these institutions. There is room for selective colleges to develop curricula and pedagogies that respond to students from a variety of backgrounds, but dramatic inequalities in the environments students grow up in create differences in preparation for college that cannot be wished away. This is so in large measure because of a highly unequal pre-college education system and an economic system that starves too many families of the resources they need to support their children's success. Moreover, older students, who are disproportionately first-generation students and come from lower-income and nonwhite households, are much less likely than recent high school graduates to be able to take advantage of the residential campuses that are the norm at the more selective institutions.

If we are to expand college opportunity on a large scale, it will not be done by moving a large fraction of high school students to highly selective colleges; it will be done by improving the education at the institutions these students actually attend, before as well as during college. The vast majority of these undergraduate students attend community colleges, for-profit colleges and universities, and broad-access public universities.

From the standpoint of reducing economic inequality, the very low completion rates in broad-access institutions, including community colleges and for-profit institutions, are probably the most important issue facing American higher education. There is more to true college success than earning a credential, but completion rates at broad-access institutions are shockingly low and we must find successful strategies for increasing the share of students who accomplish their educational goals.

Among students who first enrolled at a public two-year college in 2010, one-quarter had completed a credential at that institution eight years later; the completion rate for all for-profit institutions was 37 percent, compared with 49 percent at public four-year and 60 percent at private nonprofit four-year institutions.[18] These official graduation rates do not account for the reality that many students transfer and graduate from different institutions. For example, 30 percent of students who first enrolled in a public two-year college in 2013 graduated from that institution by 2019. Another 11 percent completed a degree or certificate at a different institution.[19]

Differences by selectivity are significant. At four-year institutions, the eight-year completion rate ranged from 31 percent at open admissions institutions and 47 percent at other institutions accepting 90 percent or more of their applicants to 86 percent at those accepting less than 25 percent of their applicants. This last group of institutions enroll 1 percent of all students entering college (table 6.1).

18. U.S. Department of Education, *Digest of Education Statistics, 2019*, table 326.27.
19. Shapiro et al., *Completing College 2019 National Report*, appendix tables.

TABLE 6.1. Eight-Year Completion Rates at Starting Institution, Students First Enrolling in 2010

Completion rates are much higher at more selective colleges and universities.

	Eight-Year Completion Rate	Share of 2010 Beginning Students
Public two-year	25%	47%
For-profit	37%	9%
Public four-year	49%	32%
Private nonprofit four-year	60%	11%
Four-year		
Open admissions	31%	16%
90.0% or more accepted	47%	3%
75.0 to 89.9% accepted	56%	7%
50.0 to 74.9% accepted	60%	16%
25.0 to 49.9% accepted	68%	5%
Less than 25.0% accepted	86%	1%

Source: U.S. Department of Education, *Digest of Education Statistics, 2019*, table 326.27.
Note: According to the National Student Clearinghouse, 16 percent of students who first enrolled in 2010 completed a credential at a different institution within eight years. Shapiro et al., *Completing College: Eight Year Completion Outcomes for the Fall 2010 Cohort*, figure 1.

It would, as we have said, be good to see selective colleges and universities enroll and graduate more students from diverse backgrounds. That would be good for the institutions, good for society, and very good for the students involved. But such efforts will only touch a small fraction of the students who graduate from high school every year, or who return to school as adults, with the ambition of earning a degree.

For many students with poor high school records, it makes economic sense to enroll in a postsecondary program—provided they have a reasonable chance of success. An associate degree with vocational dimension is likely to more than pay for itself in extra earnings, albeit the gains are relatively modest compared to a BA. Even relatively small earnings increments can make a real difference in the standard of living of households with incomes below the median. And students who transfer to four-year programs after completing associate degrees are as likely to earn bachelor's degrees as those who begin at a four-year institution. Some, but not all, programs that lead to a vocational certificate instead of a degree are also worth the investment in economic terms. Still, the most significant gains are achieved by students who graduate with a bachelor's degree: graduates can expect to be earning $20,000 to $30,000 more per year than high school graduates for as long as they continue to work. And that calculation ignores the other personal and social benefits such education yields.

But economically, trying college really only makes sense if you do have a reasonable chance at success. Time in college is costly for students, in time away from the labor market as well as in money they pay from earnings, loans, or other sources for college expenses. Many students, especially low-income, minority, and first-generation students, are being poorly treated in the educational system we have. People with these backgrounds often emerge from weak elementary and secondary schools only to find that the college options accessible to them offer little prospect of success. A big part of the solution to this problem has to be more effective investment in the social and educational development of youth from the earliest ages.

But that agenda, urgent and important as it is, is no help for students who have already completed high school. Thus, another urgent—and more immediate—challenge, given a precollege system that is failing so many of its neediest students, is to develop a postsecondary education system that can provide a more meaningful opportunity for further education for people who have not fared well in earlier education—a group that includes many older adults returning to college to improve their labor market opportunities.

Improving the prospects for these students also increases the chances that their children will begin their lives in more favorable circumstances. It is probably fair to say that for some decades after community colleges became widespread, political and educational leaders did not attach a high priority to solving the problem of community college success. Students who were not judged to be "college material" after high school could always try community college if they wanted to, and if it didn't work out, well, there were plenty of acceptable jobs around for people with high school degrees.[20] The fact that community college enrollees are and have been disproportionately Black and brown no doubt reinforced negative judgments about investing in them in a society dominated by Whites.[21] Indeed, worrying about the problem of high school dropouts, who were far more prevalent in the last half of the twentieth century than they are now, captured more attention.[22]

This complacent view about college completion has become less and less tenable as the job prospects for high school graduates continue to dwindle, as college experience has become more and more of a social norm, and as disadvantaged populations have become increasingly interested in earning college degrees. Philanthropists, researchers, and policy analysts have had promoting more college success, especially for historically underserved populations, squarely in their sights for more than a decade now, and indeed there has been progress.

20. Clark, "The 'Cooling-Out' Function in Higher Education."

21. Alesina, Glaeser, and Sacerdote, "Why Doesn't the United States Have a European-Style Welfare State?"

22. The high school completion rate (measured as the percentage of 18- to 24-year-olds with a high school degree) went from 83 percent in 1972 to 94 percent in 2018. U.S. Department of Education, *Digest of Education Statistics, 2019*, table 219.65.

For example, the share of students beginning at public four-year colleges and universities who completed a degree anywhere within six years rose from 60.6 percent for the 2006 enrolling cohort to 66.7 percent for the 2013 cohort. For community college students, the increase was from 36.3 percent to 40.8 percent.[23]

But progress has been slow. A number of strategies have the potential to improve outcomes.

Provide Guidance

Students need substantial guidance in making decisions about whether and where to go to college and how to finance it. Government websites such as College Navigator and College Scorecard contain a wealth of information about prices, aid, completion rates, debt levels, and other important issues. But they are not easy for vulnerable students to access or understand. And many students need personal guidance to make decisions about which programs and institutions are most appropriate for them. Immediate high school graduates at least have high school guidance counselors, although these professionals are often overwhelmed with students and may have little training in college advising as such. Adults coming to college—in recent years, often from the military—lack even that advising resource. The choices between attending a community college or a for-profit college, of whether to pursue an academic or a vocational path, and of whether and how much to borrow toward college expenses are critical. Students from first-generation college families are particularly vulnerable to poor or absent advice. Often,

---

23. Shapiro et al., *Completing College 2019 National Report*. These figures differ from those in table 6.1, which measures only completion at the institutions in which students first enroll.

students find themselves getting their advice from the college they wind up attending, and particularly but not only in the case of for-profit colleges, the advice they get may be aligned better with the institution's than the student's interests. This is an area where we believe government regulation is warranted, a point we will return to in chapter 7, which addresses government's role in promoting greater equity in the higher education system.

Improve Pre-College Preparation

Colleges that admit students from a broad range of academic backgrounds have to grapple with the fact that many of their students will not be well prepared to tackle the demands of college courses, either in particular areas or sometimes across the board. Selective colleges often manage this challenge by simply declining to admit students who have these limitations, but obviously that is not an option for places with open admissions. Some broad-access institutions have built relationships with high schools in their catchment areas, working with faculty to help them help their students to be ready for the coursework at that college. Many community colleges work with local school districts to run early college high schools that provide students with a rigorous curriculum and the opportunity to accumulate credits and be prepared for college.[24]

In addition, an increasing number of students are completing some college courses through dual enrollment programs while they are in high school. In 2015–16, almost 30 percent of undergraduate students 23 or younger had taken college-level

24. Texas is an example of a state with a large early college high school program. See Texas Education Agency, "Early College High School."

courses other than through the Advanced Placement (AP) or International Baccalaureate (IB) programs. Participation rates ranged from 24 percent of traditional-age Black students to 31 percent of White students.[25] In fall 2010, 15 percent of students enrolling in community colleges were high school students. Those who continued at community colleges after completing high school had higher completion rates than other community college students.[26]

Improve Practices Surrounding "Remediation"

Traditionally, broad-access colleges have tried to meet the challenge of poorly prepared students through a kind of triage process. Students take placement exams on entry and, depending on their scores, are assigned to separate "remedial" or "developmental" courses they have to pass before being allowed into the regular college courses in a particular field. These courses don't earn college credit, but for needy students, they do use up semesters of Pell Grant eligibility. Unfortunately, these placement exams have proved not to be very good at distinguishing students who would or would not succeed at regular courses, with the result that some students are needlessly set back while others are in over their heads.[27] Remedial courses can work well for students who are in need of a refresher on material they once learned, but it is no surprise that students who couldn't get through algebra in high school often don't succeed in passing a

25. U.S. Department of Education, *National Postsecondary Student Aid Study, 2016.*

26. Fink, Jenkins, and Yanagiura, *What Happens to Students Who Take Community College "Dual Enrollment" Courses in High School?*

27. Scott-Clayton, "Do High-Stakes Placement Exams Predict College Success?"

similar course on a college campus (where being assigned to the course is itself a reminder of earlier failure). The evidence is that students who are assigned to multiple remedial courses on entry to a community college have a low probability of graduating, and many never succeed in earning any college credit.[28]

Recently, a number of broad-access institutions have experimented with more imaginative and constructive ways to tackle this challenge. One promising approach is "co-requisite remediation," with students registering for the regular college course while simultaneously taking supplementary classwork in areas where their skills are weak. Introducing the remedial work at just the point in the course where it is needed helps students see the purpose and put their new learning to work right away. Another strategy is to rethink the curriculum of remedial classes, highlighting the career relevance of a subject like writing or math. Students may find probability and statistics a more engaging subject than algebra, for example.

Considering a wider range of evidence on preparation—notably students' high school records rather than only placement tests—can better identify students who need remediation in order to succeed in college-level coursework. Providing support systems, including access to childcare for students who are parents, is also a critical component of supporting student success.

None of these approaches or others that are being tried are magic bullets, but they all show a willingness on the part of educational institutions to share ownership of the problem of helping students succeed. This outlook is essential to progress. All these efforts add to the costs of education both for the students and the

28. Scott-Clayton and Rodriguez, "Development, Discouragement, or Diversion?"; Scott-Clayton, Crosta, and Belfield, "Improving the Targeting of Treatment."

colleges, at institutions that are very often strapped for funds, a point we will return to.[29]

Clarify Pathways to College Success

Another major challenge that has recently been in the spotlight for community colleges is posed by the many-sided missions of these institutions. They take seriously their responsibility to respond to the full range of community needs. Almost half of community college students are in noncredit programs that do not lead to degrees or certificates.[30] Courses may range from Shakespeare and calculus to pipe fitting and welding to meditation and dog grooming. Students include young men and women right out of high school, retirees studying conversational French, and newly arrived immigrants learning English as a second language. LaGuardia College in New York prepares students for citizenship tests. Community colleges often work closely with local industry in training workers on a contract basis.

These varied commitments can make community colleges exciting places and powerful assets for their communities, as James and Deborah Fallows have explained in their book *Our Towns*. But this complexity can pose a real challenge for students who need to focus on their own distinctive mission: to earn an associate degree or certificate and move on to either a bachelor's degree or the workforce. Particularly for first-generation college students, any type of college presents a confusing landscape, and it is all too easy to get lost. But precisely because community colleges accommodate people with so

29. Le et al., *Expanding Pathways to College Enrollment and Degree Attainment*. See also Rutschow et al., *The Changing Landscape of Developmental Education Practices*.

30. American Association of Community Colleges, *Fast Facts 2020*.

many different goals, and because these colleges are so strapped for funds to provide advice and guidance for students, the challenge for them is particularly great. Students faced with this complex set of choices and operating in an environment with little by way of advisement can easily wander around, trying this and trying that but lacking a focused aim. Wanting to move downstream toward completion, they find themselves, in Judith Scott-Clayton's apt metaphor, floating in a "shapeless river."[31]

A promising framework for addressing this challenge is to take a "guided pathways" approach to students' education.[32] The idea is to present newly arriving degree-seeking students with a set of pathways that will help them set a course toward degree completion. Starting at a broad level, orienting a student toward, say, a STEM program or a communications program, the pathway will then proceed to offer branches term by term—STEM might articulate into computer technology or biomedical work and proceed from there. Intensive (or "intrusive," as it is sometimes called) advising helps make sure course selections stay on track. Students who are not succeeding on their chosen track receive prompt feedback. Part of the great potential—but also one of the major challenges—for the guided pathways approach is that it requires the active participation of faculty. Curricula need to be thought through from the standpoint of moving students along a designed path; course content and pedagogy may also need revision in order to align skill building and course content along a coherent path. Faculty quite predictably tend to become attached to their familiar practices and outlooks and are jealous of their autonomy. But many valuable changes require active cooperation and sometimes leadership from faculty. Although the use of some

31. Scott-Clayton, "The Shapeless River."
32. Bailey, Jaggars, and Jenkins, *Redesigning America's Community Colleges.*

of these innovations is too new for definitive measures of effectiveness, they are a promising strategy for addressing a fundamental need. And there is strong evidence pointing to the effectiveness of personalized advising services.[33] All of these things cost money.

Conclusion

The United States has a highly decentralized system of higher education. A great deal of decision-making authority, even in individual institutions that are part of public systems, is delegated to the campus level. Some institutions, especially those with large financial endowments, have a larger range of options than others. In this chapter we have identified goals and practices institutions with different roles and resources can adopt to make greater contributions to promoting economic equality and opportunity among their students and more broadly.

As significant as actions by individual colleges can be, we must also recognize the potential value of collective action by coalitions of institutions. Coordinating transfer among colleges—a problem much harder than it looks—is a simple example. Just imagine the dimensions of the challenge of identifying which courses at a single California community college have an equivalent counterpart at each of the nine University of California campuses. One researcher has estimated that anyone attempting such a comparison would need to examine roughly 63 million pairs of courses. And that's for just one of 110 California community college campuses. This is a coordination problem that can only be resolved either by enforced conformity across all the institutions

---

33. Bettinger and Baker, "The Effects of Student Coaching"; Center for Community College Student Engagement, *Show Me the Way*.

of the widely dispersed and highly differentiated California public higher education system (hard to imagine) or by artificial intelligence and machine learning (now being attempted).[34]

Coordinated action may be particularly important in encouraging colleges to break down patterns of established privilege that run counter to equalizing opportunity. It may be difficult for an individual college or university with an established practice of legacy admissions to abandon it—although Johns Hopkins University (which was the beneficiary not long ago of an unusually large donation) recently made this change. It is less far-fetched to picture a group of institutions jointly agreeing to eliminate these admission preferences or reduce their importance. Elite colleges might also be able to agree on cost-cutting measures, perhaps through the use of technology, that would free resources for helping disadvantaged students. Any one institution taking this step might lose competitive advantage; this would be less of an issue if a set of respected institutions acted together. That option, however, is limited by concerns about anti-trust restrictions.

In other words, both individual institutions and groups of institutions, even with ambitious goals related to reducing inequality, are constrained in the range of actions they can undertake. Still, virtually all colleges and universities in the United States get a significant share of their resources from governments, either directly through appropriations or indirectly through federal student aid. They have a clear responsibility to act in the social interest. All institutions—public, private nonprofit, and for-profit—are also subject to oversight and regulation from government agencies. In the next chapter we examine the roles that governments now play and could play in shaping inequality and opportunity in higher education.

34. Pardos, Chau, and Zhao, "Data-Assistive Course-to-Course Articulation."

CHAPTER 7
Policy Directions

Chapter 6 focused on how academic institutions—both elite institutions and broad-access institutions—can do more to help solve these problems. We argued that improving the capacity of broad-access colleges and universities to provide high-quality educational opportunities to the large numbers of low- and moderate-income students who do—and will continue to—attend these institutions is the most critical issue.

In this chapter, we address the public policy context in which colleges and universities operate. Before delving into specific policies, it is worth keeping in mind some of the basic truths about investment in higher education.

- Higher education spending, like all education spending, is an investment in improving human lives in both economic and broader social terms.
- These investments have to be paid for, and shifting costs from one payer to another does not make college "free." The key questions are: Is the funding adequate? Is the money being well spent? And is it being spent at the

places and on the people where it will do the most good, for those individuals and for society? Are people being shut out of educational opportunities because of their limited financial resources?

- Investments in higher education tend to pay off well, in both narrower financial and broader social terms. The problem of "affordability" of college both for individuals and for society looks very different when thought about as present investment for future gain instead of as a consumption item like an expensive vacation.

- In the near term, a lot of attention and money need to be directed toward people who have been let down by the educational and social systems of this nation at earlier points in their lives. These investments are worth making both for the sake of the individuals involved and for the sake of future generations. We should be mindful, though, that the need for such "remedial" or "compensatory" investments can be reduced over time if we invest consistently in improved education at earlier ages. It's not for nothing that a major nonprofit organization promoting high-quality early childhood education was named "An Ounce of Prevention."[1]

---

1. Better education before college may or may not lead to less spending on education after high school. Students who are better prepared for college get more out of it and are likely to go to college longer. We would expect to see more people completing bachelor's degrees and fewer people dropping out of school with no credential if pre-college education gets better. In fact, the evidence in health care is that disease prevention does more to improve people's quality and length of life than it does to save costs within the health care sector. See Carroll, "Preventive Care Saves Money?"

Higher Education Policy in the Context of Pre-College Inequality

As noted throughout this book, variation in students' higher education experiences reflects, in large measure, the sharp differences in pre-college opportunity experienced by children with different backgrounds. For example, community colleges and for-profit institutions, which generally admit any student with a high school degree (as well as some without that credential), disproportionately enroll students from low-income families, those whose parents do not have college degrees, and children from historically disadvantaged racial and ethnic groups. Highly selective colleges and universities, both public and private, are designed around the aim of advancing the education of students who are prepared to succeed in an academically demanding environment. In a society where only a limited segment of the population grows up in circumstances that support such preparation, it is no surprise that highly selective institutions disproportionately enroll students from families with higher-income and more-educated parents and, despite efforts to promote diversity, enroll relatively few Black and Hispanic students.

In the United States about 60 percent of postsecondary students—but only 30 percent of dependent students whose parents' incomes are $250,000 or higher—start out at community colleges. Between 5 and 10 percent begin at for-profit institutions.

About 5 percent of Americans—but a quarter of those from families with incomes of $250,000 or higher—begin their studies at a highly selective college or university, one that admits fewer than 25 percent of its applicants. Students at these institutions are much more likely to graduate than students enrolling elsewhere, consistent with the fact that these students are carefully selected for their ability to succeed in school. And affluent parents are much better situated to put money into developing their kids' talents and fostering their abilities in a variety of ways.

The majority of students enrolling at public or private nonprofit four-year colleges and universities go to moderately or minimally selective colleges, with most of the enrollment at public campuses such as California State University or other non-flagship publics.

The sorting of students into these different categories of colleges is far more a reflection of differences in preparation for college than of differences in ability to pay at the time of enrollment. Paying for college is, of course, a major hurdle for many students. But it is the differential ability of families to provide for their children's college preparation throughout their earlier lives, not for their college tuition, that matters most. As economists Pedro Carneiro and James Heckman have shown, it is families' incomes over their children's growing-up years that matter most for their educational outcomes.[2]

The substantial differences in preparation for college generated by variation in pre-college experiences make it unavoidable that people from different backgrounds will have different types of college experiences that will shape their later lives, reinforcing earlier inequalities. And the differences in the job opportunities available after people leave the education system are widened by the way that post-college labor markets operate and the dramatic gaps in compensation for different kinds of work. The vital task of improving higher education policy and practice operates within these constraints.

---

2. Carneiro and Heckman, "The Evidence on Credit Constraints in Post-Secondary Schooling."

These realities do not diminish the importance of postsecondary institutions renewing and rethinking their efforts to educate students from diverse backgrounds. As discussed in the preceding chapter, highly selective institutions should reconsider their admissions and aid policies; moderately selective public and private universities and colleges need to sustain a focus on high-quality undergraduate education even under the pressures of tightening budgets and demanding research commitments; broad-access institutions should redouble their efforts to gain access to more public resources and develop strategies to use those resources more effectively. And all institutions should make student success a top priority.

In this chapter we review directions for state and federal policies relating to higher education that show promise for increasing the number of individuals for whom higher education is a transformative experience bringing economic security, personal satisfaction, and stronger citizenship. Both the individuals directly affected and society as a whole will benefit from a better-educated population with more widespread personal autonomy and capacity for contributing politically, socially, and economically. Moreover, as we have noted repeatedly, increasing the share of adults with high-quality college degrees will change the balance of supply and demand, reducing the earnings of college graduates relative to others—and thereby reducing economic inequality.

Focus on Quality, Not Only on Price

Public pressure to focus on lowering the price of college without attending to what students actually get for that price is a powerful influence on both lawmakers and administrators. National policies must counter this short-sighted view, which focuses on who pays the bill instead of on what is being purchased.

The quality of the postsecondary experience is at the top of our priority list because it is so neglected in the public discourse. No matter how low the price, students will not be well served by programs and institutions that do not provide the guidance, support, and learning opportunities they need to achieve their goals. The primary responsibility of most colleges and universities and of most faculty is undergraduate teaching, and it is important that this work be done well.[3]

The almost exclusive focus on costs and prices has led to disproportionate attention on two types of innovations on which many observers and participants have pinned their hopes for increasing access to affordable higher education. We are pessimistic about the potential for "free" and "debt-free" college proposals to significantly reduce inequality of educational outcomes because of the focus on what people pay—and on messaging about what people pay—and the lack of focus on the resources available to colleges and universities and the quality of the experiences they offer.

We are also skeptical about the short-term prospects for fully online postsecondary courses and programs to narrow the gaps across students from different backgrounds—and to significantly lower the cost of providing the experiences at-risk students need to succeed. The coronavirus pandemic dramatically increased the role of online learning and as of this writing, it is impossible to predict how lasting that impact will be. In any case, we are not optimistic that this experience will do much to mitigate the reality that students without strong academic preparation struggle most with learning environments that do not

3. Baum and McPherson, "Improving Teaching."

involve significant personal interaction among students, their classmates, and their instructors.

These changes that sound as though they have the potential to be game changers might end up exacerbating, rather than diminishing, inequalities. Before detailing the kinds of efforts that are more promising, we discuss these two ideas that have gained so much attention as potential cure-alls. "Free college" is prominent in state and federal policy conversations. Increased reliance on purely online learning is, in some respects, an institutional decision. However, public policies have considerable influence in this arena through both financial aid systems and regulatory approaches.

Technology as Savior

The reliance on technology to reduce the cost of educating large numbers of students appears, at least to date, to be a disappointing innovation. The idea is that it will be cheaper to provide education online than in person and that the technology will make it easier for students who have limited time and are not geographically mobile to access education. But evidence suggests that lowering costs by going online is not so simple. Of even greater concern, students with weak academic backgrounds are less successful in purely online courses than when they have in-person contact with faculty and other students— and format makes more difference for these students than for those with stronger academic preparation.

Some online courses do require that all students participate at the same time and interact remotely with a faculty member. This kind of online education played a large role during the pandemic, mostly through the use of Zoom. But it is quite costly and is unlikely to remain widespread after safety concerns about in-person classes fade. The varieties of fully online education that are cheapest and easiest to scale are asynchronous, allowing students to log in whenever and wherever it is most convenient. For full-time workers, parents, and others with many demands on their time, this convenience could make postsecondary study a realistic option. The same is true of potential students who live far from a college offering the curriculum they are seeking. When the alternatives are online or nothing, online may be better, just as in earlier generations correspondence courses were a needed "second-best" for those in remote places.

And teaching more students with fewer instructors can make a big dent in the cost of providing higher education. Rather than paying three professors on campus to lecture in halls seating a hundred students each, a university can pay one professor to give one lecture reaching an indefinitely large number of students at the same time. (This was the idea underlying the Massive Open Online Courses [MOOC] movement that for a moment people thought would transform higher education.) Beyond the lecture approach, students can access prepackaged online courses with exercises that allow them to progress at their own pace, relieving faculty members of repeated interactions with individuals and small groups.

Putting lectures and simple materials online can be done without a big investment. Eliminating the need for classroom space and other physical facilities is a cost-saver. Institutions where a large share of students are studying exclusively online charge slightly lower prices than similar institutions with more programs involving face-to-face contact. But that saving does not carry over to programs that are only partially online (so-called "hybrid" courses).[4]

---

4. Deming et al., "Can Online Learning Bend the Higher Education Cost Curve?"

And it turns out that high-quality online courses are expensive to deliver—at least as expensive, if not more, to develop and staff as traditional face-to-face instruction. Moreover, updating online courses can come at significant cost.[5]

In other words, at least for now, a focus on using technology to minimize costs (and potentially prices for students) is likely to lead to large-scale, simple, easy-to-produce programs. It is not likely to generate creative, personalized, up-to-date courses that are elements of programs that involve a mix of online and face-to-face interactions.

The type and quality of online learning accessible to students—especially those with limited academic preparation and limited resources—are critical. Mounting evidence suggests that although the outcomes of hybrid learning environments that mix online and classroom experiences are similar to those of traditional classrooms,[6] the same is not true of purely online courses.

Online students are older, have lower levels of parental education, are more likely to be single parents, and are more likely to be working full time while enrolled in school than are other college students.[7] Several studies using rigorous experimental techniques have found that while, on average, grades and other outcomes measures are only slightly lower for purely online courses, the disadvantages of online courses are greater for less-prepared students and for Hispanic students. Students who take online classes appear to do less well in subsequent courses and are more likely than others to drop out of school.[8]

5. McPherson and Bacow, "Online Higher Education."

6. Alpert, Couch, and Harmon, "A Randomized Assessment of Online Learning"; Bowen et al., "Interactive Learning Online at Public Universities."

7. Deming et al., "Can Online Learning Bend the Higher Education Cost Curve?"

8. Figlio, Rush, and Yin, "Is It Live or Is It Internet?"; Figlio, "A Silver Lining for Online Higher Education?"; Escueta et al., "Education Technology"; Bettinger and

Online courses, particularly those where students can do the work on their own schedules, may require more self-discipline, time-management skills, and confidence than needed in traditional classroom courses. They are also likely to limit opportunities for networking and interacting with peers, mentors, and instructors, potentially hampering the educational process.[9] Charles Isbell, one of the architects of the celebrated Georgia Tech online master's program in computer science, remarked at a conference in 2018 that the main reason students fail in the program is not technical skill but "isolation." The absence of colleagues who visibly struggle and of mentors who encourage effort is just too much for some students.[10] These realities make it unsurprising that students without strong academic skills and preparation struggle without the classroom structure.

Some of the better news about online programs comes from efforts targeting students who have already proved their ability to succeed in advanced academic work. The Georgia Tech program mentioned just above is getting very positive reviews and appears to be opening opportunities to new students rather than diverting them from face-to-face programs.[11] Since this is a graduate program at an elite engineering university, all of the students have already earned strong bachelor's degrees. Evidence about success in MOOCs confirms the reality that

Loeb, "Promises and Pitfalls of Online Education"; Dynarski, "Online Courses Are Harming the Students Who Need the Most Help."

9. Escueta et al., "Education Technology."

10. Remarks at the William G. Bowen Colloquium, October 25, 2018, Washington, DC.

11. Goodman, Melkers, and Pallais, "Can Online Delivery Increase Access to Education?"

students from higher-income, more educated backgrounds are most likely to participate and succeed in MOOCs.[12]

In fall 2018, 17 percent of degree-seeking undergraduate students were in online-only programs; 35 percent took at least some of their classes online. But 63 percent of all students enrolled in for-profit institutions—open-access institutions that disproportionately enroll low-income, Black, and Hispanic students—were studying entirely online.[13] Virtually no students at highly selective institutions were in fully online programs. Non-selective public and private nonprofit colleges and universities and independent for-profits fell between these extremes.[14] In other words, it is the students for whom face-to-face learning environments are most critical who are most likely to be taking their coursework online.

The pandemic our nation and the world was living through as we were writing this book highlighted a further difficulty with purely online instructional programs. When students are forced by social distancing needs to stay away from classrooms, they are for the most part thrown on their own (or their parents') resources to fashion an environment for learning. As is true of so much of what happened in the pandemic, this necessity made more visible the enormous inequality in the resources and affordances of the daily lives of Americans with different economic, social, and racial-ethnic backgrounds. Most directly, there is huge variation in the quality and availability of high-speed internet connections and capable computers for students in different living situations. Beyond that, though, there are

12. Waddell, "Virtual Classrooms Can Be as Unequal as Real Ones."

13. U.S. Department of Education, *Digest of Education Statistics, 2019*, table 311.15.

14. Deming et al., "Can Online Learning Bend the Higher Education Cost Curve?"

questions about availability of quiet places to study (and participate in Zoom calls), coping with family responsibilities, and practicing needed types of self-care. Researchers have only begun studying the implications of all this variation, but we already know that the variation is large and is quite likely to prove consequential. (A research team led by Richard Arum at the University of California-Irvine is taking advantage of studies already underway there to develop systematic evidence on these questions.)[15]

Technology is likely to progress and strategies for improving learning outcomes in online courses will surely emerge. Some courses seem to lend themselves more readily than others to partial or even total technology-based instruction and including them in primarily in-person programs could lead to cost savings. And certainly, some students, particularly older students with work and family responsibilities and those in rural areas, may be choosing between purely online education or no postsecondary education at all. But there is a real risk that both cost-cutting efforts and well-intentioned moves to expand access to higher education could lead to greater numbers of disadvantaged students being relegated to cheap and ineffective online instruction.

As Michael McPherson and Lawrence Bacow argue:

> If technology is used in broad-access institutions to drive cost down without regard to quality, and at the same time is used in elite higher education to further increase the cost and restrict the availability of the "best" education, we will wind up with a society both more unequal and less productive

---

15. An overview of the broader study from which this effort flows is Burke, "Assessing the Value of an Undergrad Degree."

than it could be. If the new digital technology is used in broad-access institutions to extend education to a wider population and in top-level institutions to reduce the cost and expand the availability of exceptionally good education to more of those who can benefit from it, we can view the future with more optimism.[16]

State and federal governments should design polices that recognize the risks of purely online coursework designed to reduce costs. Participation in publicly funded financial aid programs should require meaningful interaction between students and faculty, as well as reliable standards for student outcomes. State regulations can also incorporate safeguards against institutions designing low-quality academic programs. Medical practitioners invoke "do no harm" as a first principle. But colleges that waste students' and society's money and time on programs that graduate a tiny share of students, or that send them off with credentials that have no value, can easily leave students worse off than when they arrived. We should not tolerate such programs. The federal government should revisit the Obama administration's Gainful Employment rule and develop a strong system for excluding the lowest-performing institutions from the federal student aid system.

Free College as Panacea

A second example would be a panacea for increasing educational opportunity that could end up widening the gaps between the haves and the have-nots is "free college." In this case, the goal is not to lower the *cost* of producing education but simply to lower

16. McPherson and Bacow, "Online Higher Education," 17.

the *price* students must pay. That is, the aim is to shift the cost away from students and families to some (often unspecified) other people who will pay the cost instead.

Tuition prices have increased much more rapidly over time than prices of most other goods and services. Paying for college is a challenge for all but the most affluent students and families, particularly because it is very difficult to both go to school full time and work full time. So, students generally don't have the earnings needed to support a reasonable standard of living.

Low-income households have trouble paying for lots of things. There is broad consensus that society has some responsibility for making sure that people have enough to eat and a roof over their heads—even if the policies designed to address these problems don't go as far as many people think they should. But there is no movement to make food and housing free.

As it has become more and more difficult to earn a living wage—or at least a wage that can support a family above the poverty level—without a postsecondary credential, a college education has moved from the optional side of the ledger to the list of goods and services to which everyone should have access.

An obvious remedy for prices that don't fit into most household budgets is to find a way to lower tuition. And the most appealing tuition price to many is zero. Why should there be any price tag that creates a barrier to individuals seeking to invest in themselves and their futures, particularly when that investment has spillover benefits that increase the health and wealth of society as a whole, in addition to raising the incomes of college graduates?

Advocates of free public college often note that public education through high school is free. But several factors differentiate college from earlier levels of education. First, school attendance is compulsory and is provided to minor children who cannot be allowed to decide for themselves whether to participate. Second, the requirement for attendance at school rests on the fact that basic verbal and quantitative skills are needed to allow people to communicate with one another for a workable democratic society. These are public benefits, which bear some analogy to requirements for mask-wearing in a pandemic. Higher education, as we have argued, provides public benefits too, but the private benefits are a more important part of the equation, especially in a more advanced society. Finally, as we show in chapter 4, making public education free by no means ensures that it will be equal either in terms of resource distribution or in the quality of the opportunities it provides to people with different backgrounds.

Most proposals for free college are limited to public institutions. Students choosing to enroll in private (nonprofit or for-profit) colleges and universities would still pay tuition. Presumably, fewer students would make that choice. But even within the public sector, as discussed in chapter 4, there are significant differences in enrollment patterns by family income. We would be providing a year or two of free community college—now averaging $3,770 per year before financial aid—to many low-income students and four years free at a flagship public university—now averaging $11,440 a year—to many higher-income students.[17]

There is no doubt that paying for college takes an increasing share of household income—both because college prices have risen so rapidly and because incomes have stagnated. In 1980, the average tuition and fee price at public four-year colleges was $3,510 (in 2019 dollars) and median income for families with

17. Ma, Pender, and Libassi, *Trends in College Pricing, 2020.*

TABLE 7.1. Changes in Median Family Income and College Tuition over Time

Average public college tuition has tripled, while median family income has
increased very little over 30 years.

	Median Family Income Ages 45–54 in 2019 Dollars	10-Year % Change	Average Public Four-Year College Tuition and Fees in 2019 Dollars	10-Year % Change
1989	$92,031		$3,510	
1999	$100,477	9%	$5,170	47%
2009	$90,430	−10%	$8,420	63%
2019	$108,609	20%	$10,440	24%
Change 1989–2019	$16,578	18%		197%

Source: U.S. Census Bureau, Historical Income Tables, Families, table F-11; Ma et al., Trends in
College Pricing, 2019.

householders between the ages of 45 and 54 was $92,031. A de-
cade later, tuition was 47 percent higher, after adjusting for inflation, and median income was 9 percent higher. Tuition rose
63 percent between 1999 and 2009, at the same time that median income fell by 10 percent. Median income recovered, rising
by 20 percent over the next decade, and was $108,609 in 2019,
but during those years tuition rose by another 24 percent. Over
thirty years, public four-year college tuition tripled after adjusting for inflation, but median family income grew just 18 percent.
It is no wonder families are struggling trying to figure out how
to pay for their children's education.

So, wouldn't eliminating tuition go far toward equalizing access to college, making it as easy for low- and middle-income
students to pay as it is for their affluent peers? Tempting as it is,
this idea ignores a number of realities:

1) *Tuition and fees account for a small share of the expenses
   most students must cover when they are in college.* They
   must also buy books and supplies and find a way to pay

for the things their earnings would cover if they spent their time in a job instead of in school: rent, food, transportation, and so on. For example, the average full-time student at a public four-year institution had a total estimated budget of $26,590 in 2019–20. Tuition and fees accounted for 39 percent of that amount. Non-tuition expenses accounted for 80 percent of the average community college budget.[18] Free tuition doesn't cover these expenses. Low-income students need their Pell Grants (which can be used for living expenses)—and more—even if tuition is free.

2) *Many low- and moderate-income students already receive grant aid that covers their tuition and fees—making college as "free" as it would be under a "free college" policy.* Relatively few families with students at public four-year institutions pay the full tuition. In 2015–16, two-thirds of full-time dependent students with family income between $63,000 and $113,499 per year received some form of grant aid or tuition discount, and even a majority of those with incomes higher than that get some help.[19] More than 80 percent of dependent students at public two-year colleges with family incomes below $35,000 received enough grant aid to cover their entire tuition and required fees. The same was true for more than half of the independent students (those whose parental income is not in the financial picture because they are older, are married, have dependent children, are veterans, or are in other related circumstances) enrolled in

18. Ma et al., *Trends in College Pricing, 2019.*
19. Authors' calculation from the U.S. Department of Education, *National Postsecondary Student Aid Study, 2016.*

TABLE 7.2. Distribution of Full-Time Undergraduate Students at Public Institutions by Net Tuition and Fees, 2015–16

Many low-income students have all or most of their tuition and required fees covered by grant aid.

		Public Two-Year			
	$0	$1 to $2,499	$2,500 to $4,999	$5,000 to $7,499	$7,500 or Higher
All	52%	22%	17%	5%	3%
Independent students (34%)	56%	20%	17%	5%	3%
Dependent students (66%)	50%	23%	18%	6%	3%
Dependent students: parents' income					
Less than $35,000 (36%)	81%	8%	7%	3%	1%
$35,000 to $69,999 (29%)	44%	30%	17%	6%	2%
$70,000 to $119,999 (24%)	22%	33%	31%	9%	6%
$120,000 or higher (12%)	24%	31%	28%	8%	8%

		Public Four-Year			
	$0	$1 to $4,999	$5,000 to $9,999	$10,000 to $19,999	$20,000 or Higher
All	28%	23%	26%	18%	5%
Independent students (17%)	29%	31%	26%	12%	2%
Dependent students (83%)	27%	21%	26%	20%	6%
Dependent students: parents' income					
Less than $35,000 (26%)	58%	25%	10%	5%	1%
$35,000 to $69,999 (21%)	32%	29%	24%	12%	2%
$70,000 to $119,999 (25%)	13%	20%	37%	25%	6%
$120,000 or higher (28%)	8%	12%	32%	34%	14%

Source: Ma et al., Trends in College Pricing, 2018, figure 11.

these institutions. The shares with "free" tuition were lower at public four-year institutions, but for most low-income students, net tuition and fee prices were much lower than the published prices. However, in the absence of a clear announcement, many prospective students do not understand that they will not have to pay tuition.

3) *Many public institutions, particularly those that enroll large numbers of low-income students, are underfunded and struggle to provide the academic and social supports students need to succeed.* If they do not have tuition revenues, they will need considerable additional revenues from another source to offer educational opportunities of reasonable quality. As noted in chapter 6, among students who began at a community college in fall 2013, only 41 percent had completed a postsecondary credential at any institution six years later. Almost half had no credential and were no longer enrolled.[20] If more students enroll in community colleges because they know it will be "free," the pressures on these institutions will increase and we are likely to increase the number of disadvantaged people who have tried college, possibly accumulating debt along the way, and have little or nothing to show for it.

4) *If students and families do not contribute to the cost of education, someone else will have to pay.* Presumably this would be taxpayers at either the state or federal level. Raising taxes is not a popular idea. But if taxes did go up, families would have less after-tax income to pay for college. They would, however, be more generously subsidized by other taxpayers—including those without a college education who have relatively low incomes. A possible response is that the needed money will come from higher taxes on the very rich. But our

20. Shapiro et al., *Completing College: A National View of Student Completion Rates—Fall 2011 Cohort.*

country has many spending priorities—including reducing the inequality of the circumstances in which children grow up and are educated, as well as spending more money on the education of students at underfunded colleges—and so the question of how high a priority this use of money is can't be sidestepped.

As detailed in chapter 3, people who grow up in relatively affluent households are most likely to go to college. When they go to college, they are most likely to go to four-year colleges and particularly to selective, flagship, or doctoral institutions whose students benefit from higher resources than students at two-year and broad-access institutions. The number of years students stay in college is also correlated with income, since those from low-income backgrounds are most likely to drop out without completing their programs and if they do earn credentials, they are more likely to be short-term certificates or associate degrees—not the bachelor's degrees that are more common among those from more privileged backgrounds.

So, eliminating tuition would involve more financial relief to more rich people and smaller gifts to fewer poor people. According to an estimate from the Brookings Institution, families from the top half of the income distribution would have received 24 percent more in dollar value from eliminating tuition than students from the lower half of the income distribution under Bernie Sanders's 2016 free college plan.[21] Both differential participation rates and the fact that more affluent students tend to go to more expensive colleges for more years explain this finding.

This analysis assumed that, as Sanders proposed, students would be able to keep their current federal and state grant aid

21. Chingos, "Who Would Benefit Most from Free College?"

and use it to cover non-tuition expenses. This is a critical and expensive component of that policy proposal, and one that does *not* characterize the vast majority of free-college programs states and localities have implemented or seriously considered. Instead, these programs, following the example of the attention-getting Tennessee Promise program,[22] fill the gaps between existing grant aid and the tuition price. In 2019–20, full-time students with such limited financial resources that they are deemed unable to contribute financially to their college costs received federal Pell Grants of $6,195. Tuition and fees averaged $3,730 at community colleges and $10,440 at public four-year colleges and universities.[23] Even without considering state need-based grant aid, free community college programs were unlikely to benefit students from very low-income households. And students too wealthy to qualify for need-based aid would receive almost $4,000 more in additional funding than their low-income classmates.

Neither large-scale online learning nor eliminating tuition at public colleges is likely to be as good as it sounds, and both of them have a risk of backfiring. Low-quality online education could harm the prospects of the students who experience it, and the resource drain resulting from pushing tuition down might harm the very institutions disadvantaged students most often attend. We should keep the goal in mind: reducing the differences in opportunities and outcomes between individuals from low-income backgrounds and those with more resources. Getting more people into college without ensuring that they will have a high-quality educational environment and a significant chance of completing credentials of value will not narrow

22. See tnpromise.gov.
23. Ma et al., *Trends in College Pricing, 2019.*

the gaps between the rich and the poor. We need better options. Admittedly, they may be more complicated and harder to put on a bumper sticker.

Policy Levers for Government

State governments have substantial leverage over operations of public colleges and universities through funding mechanisms and over both public and private institutions through regulatory oversight. The federal government has only a minor role in directly operating or funding undergraduate institutions but provides major support to students both through financial aid grants and through the provision of student loans. The main source of federal regulatory authority over higher education institutions comes through the government's ability to determine an institution's eligibility for federal aid for its students, and it has delegated most of that authority to accrediting bodies.

We do not attempt here to provide a comprehensive agenda for government action but rather aim to underscore major issues and important opportunities for government to reduce financial strain on students and influence institutional actions in the interest of improved outcomes for students.

Need-Based Financial Aid: A Priority

All institutions face the problem of providing financial support to students who do not have the resources to pay tuition and fees, buy books and supplies, and support themselves (and sometimes their dependents) while they are in school.

For many institutions, federal and state financial aid funds comprise the lion's share of dollars available for this purpose. The principal federal grant program, Pell Grants, is very well targeted on low- and moderate-income students. In 2019–20, over 6.6 million students received grants averaging \$4,710 (in 2019 dollars).[24] But other federal funding aimed at helping undergraduate students and their families is less well targeted. The GI Bill provides quite substantial funding to a relatively small number of students, and it is not means-tested. In 2019, 738,000 veterans received average grants of \$15,910.[25] In fairness, the GI Bill can be seen more as compensation for public service than as an aid program. No such justification is available for federal tuition tax credits and deductions. This is a large program (about \$16.4 billion in 2020),[26] only a small share of whose dollars benefit low-income students.

Most states provide the bulk of their higher education funding in the form of general appropriations that make it possible for public institutions to operate successfully without charging students tuition prices high enough to cover the full cost of their education. But these funds provide across-the-board subsidies, not targeted subsidies that reduce the resource gaps between the privileged and the less privileged. Grant aid—if it is part of a well-designed need-based aid program—can target funds on low- and moderate-income students, reducing the inequality of available resources.

On average, states devote 14 percent of their appropriations to financial aid for students, but this share ranges from zero in New Hampshire and less than 1 percent in Montana and Hawaii to 37 percent in South Carolina and more than 25 percent in Virginia and Louisiana. These programs vary greatly in terms of their targeting on lower-income students. Twenty-nine states

24. Ma, Pender, and Libassi, *Trends in College Pricing, 2020*, table 5.
25. Ibid.
26. Office of Management and Budget, "Tax Expenditures," table 13-1.

award more than 90 percent of their state grant aid on the basis of the financial circumstances of the students, but in Arkansas, Georgia, South Dakota, and Louisiana more than 90 percent of the aid is allocated on the basis of academic achievement, not financial need.[27] Some of the largest programs, like California's and Illinois's, are quite well targeted, but other states operate aid programs whose main aim seems to be to keep students from relatively affluent families attending home-state institutions.[28]

To address inequality, states should examine their aid programs and design them to most effectively increase the share of students from the lower half of the income distribution who have the opportunity to enroll and succeed in high-quality public colleges and universities.

From the mid-1970s through 2010–11, the federal government's Leveraging Educational Assistance Program (LEAP, formerly SSIG) provided matching funds for state need-based grant aid and for a time was a stimulus to both the creation and expansion of need-based student aid programs in the states. Reviving and restructuring this program would support state efforts to achieve this goal.

Most institutions complement federal and state aid programs with grants and tuition discounts from their own funds. In 2015–16, institutional funds provided only 10 percent of the average $4,500 per student in grant aid supporting full-time students at public two-year colleges and 15 percent of $8,400 per student at for-profit institutions. Students at public four-year institutions

27. National Association of State Student Grant and Aid Programs, *49th Annual Survey Report.*

28. For a detailed view of the characteristics of state grant programs and the factors influencing their equity and effectiveness, see Urban Institute, "Building a State Financial Aid Program."

received 31 percent of their $7,300 in average grants from their institutions. In contrast, institutional funds at private nonprofit four-year colleges and universities provided three-quarters of their students' average $19,000 in total grant aid.[29]

The distribution of these grant funds is critical to student success. Both private and public institutions feel a pull toward targeting tuition discounts on students with high SAT scores or athletic prowess rather than financial need. A financially constrained institution that can spend $5,000 to attract a relatively affluent student who will pay $25,000 in tuition may be able to provide more support to low-income students than it could if it failed to enroll the student who brings resources to campus. Competitive pressures for such students can result in bidding wars between colleges, and current interpretations of anti-trust laws discourage college attempts to avoid destructive competition. But it is clear that targeting aid on low- and moderate-income students is critical to making it possible for them to enroll and succeed in college. Prioritizing institutional prestige over creating these opportunities means exacerbating educational inequality rather than reducing it.

Recommendations

States should devote a significant share of their subsidies for higher education to need-based grant programs, narrowing the gaps in resources between lower-income students and those from more affluent households. This policy supplements state funding for public institutions. Grant programs that allocate funds without regard to students' financial circumstances, focusing only on academic achievement, do not have the same impact. The political viability of aid programs that benefit large numbers of

29. Baum et al., *Trends in Student Aid, 2018*, figures 18, 19.

high-need students might be stronger if the programs were designed to reach a substantial fraction of middle-income students as well. Federal support for a matching program for such grants would also strengthen their political prospects.

At the same time, the federal government, whose Pell Grant program provides more than twice as much funding as all of the state grant programs combined, should simplify and strengthen this program and make it more generous.[30]

STUDENT LOANS

A wide range of public policy proposals attempt to address struggles with student debt. Because some view eliminating borrowing for college altogether as the ideal, it is helpful to start with an understanding of the motivation for the federal student loan program. President Lyndon Johnson included a major need-based federal student loan program in the 1965 Higher Education Act to expand opportunities for students with limited means.[31] Like investments in small businesses, education provides opportunities for people to build capacity and become more productive over the long run. It is rare to have the money up front to make these investments, but because—if well thought out—they pay off well over time, it is reasonable to repay loans out of future earnings.

Not everyone's education pays off equally well and it is not always possible to predict outcomes in advance. As a result,

30. For examples of proposals to reform the Pell program, see Rethinking Pell Grants Study Group, *Rethinking Pell Grants*; and Baum and Scott-Clayton, *Redesigning the Pell Grant Program for the Twenty-First Century*. In December 2020, Congress passed the FAFSA Simplification Act, which will implement some of the changes advocates have proposed.

31. Johnson, "Remarks at Southwest Texas State College."

despite loans working out for most students, some students are unable to repay their loans. A strong public policy will provide both the cash students need to pay the bills while they are in school and an insurance policy to protect them against unexpected weak outcomes.

Students borrow to cover living expenses, not just tuition and fees. Even if there were no tuition many students would still accumulate debt.[32] If the federal government did not make loans available on good terms, students would turn to credit cards or other private markets. Because most students do not have either collateral or strong credit histories, any loans they obtained through these channels would likely come with high interest rates and harsh terms.

The federal government plays an important role in making loans available to college students. The government getting out of the loan business would significantly diminish educational opportunities. It seems clear that if the government is going to continue to make loans to students, it would be inequitable to forgive all of the debts of those who borrowed in the past. In any case, calls to broadly forgive student debt ignore the reality that higher-income households hold disproportionate amounts of student debt because most people with high debt levels went to graduate school or at least earned bachelor's degrees.[33] Many of the people struggling with student debt borrowed a few thousand dollars and were in college for a short period of time. Perhaps if we could believe that canceling a trillion dollars or more in debt were literally a free lunch, the equity argument

32. Baum and McPherson, "'Free College' Does Not Eliminate Student Debt."
33. Households in the top 40 percent of the income distribution hold 58 percent of outstanding education debt. Those in the bottom 20 percent hold 5 percent of the debt. (Baum and Looney, "Who Owes the Most in Student Loans").

would pale in significance, but there is in fact sound reason to believe that financing loan forgiveness would compete with other potential uses of government funds, either within higher education or more widely.[34] For example, the $1.5 trillion the federal government would sacrifice if it wiped out education debt obligations could cover a Pell Grant program double its current size for about twenty-five years—likely having a significant effect on educational attainment.

A better approach to mitigating problems with student debt, which are concentrated among borrowers who left school without a degree, Black borrowers, and those who attended for-profit institutions, involves a combination of preventing students from borrowing for programs that are unlikely to serve them well and strengthening the income-driven repayment system so that loan payments are always in line with borrowers' earnings.

Recommendations

The government should strengthen the requirements for institutions and programs to be allowed to participate in federal student aid programs. A combination of metrics, including graduation rates, loan repayment rates, loan default rates, and post-college earnings, could create a system that would prevent students from borrowing to enroll in postsecondary programs with very weak outcomes.[35] The elimination of the Obama administration's Gainful Employment rule, which would have excluded programs from which too many students emerged

34. For a cogent analysis of the reasons why fiscal constraints on expanding federal spending persist even in low interest rate environments, see Furman and Summers, "A Reconsideration of Fiscal Policy in the Era of Low Interest Rates." For an explanation of the impact of debt forgiveness on the federal deficit and debt, see Baum and Marron, "What Would Forgiving Student Debt Mean for the Federal Budget?"

35. Several studies have proposed policies along these lines. See, for example, Baum and Schwartz, "Unaffordable Loans."

with debt payments too high for their earnings from participating in Title IV federal student aid, has created a vacuum in this area. Developing a new policy should be an important component of preventing future students from accumulating unmanageable education debt.

A second component of student debt reform will involve improving the loan repayment system. The United States has gradually made repayment based on income more widely available since the introduction of the income-based repayment plan in 2007. About half of all outstanding debt and a third of borrowers are currently in plans that limit their payments to affordable shares of their incomes.[36] However, there are multiple confusing plans and bureaucratic hurdles to enrolling and maintaining participation. Congress should create one income-driven plan, into which borrowers would be automatically enrolled. Withholding monthly payments through the payroll system would ease the system for borrowers and protect taxpayers. The goal should not be to minimize the amount borrowers repay but to develop a simple system that expects most borrowers to repay their debts when they are able to but forgives balances for those whose incomes do not support repayment.

Key Directions for Policy Improvement

Promoting Higher Completion Rates and Shorter Time to Degree at Institutions That Serve Disadvantaged Students

In chapter 6 we described some of the efforts that community colleges and other broad-access institutions are undertaking to increase student success. We cited evidence that programs that

36. U.S. Department of Education, "Federal Student Loan Portfolio."

raise graduation rates cost more per enrolled student. But because they significantly increase the number of students who achieve their goal of graduating from college, they cost less per graduate. There is persuasive evidence that spending more on the education of these students (who currently receive less subsidy per student than more affluent undergraduates who attend more selective public universities) pays off in higher graduation rates.

These "broad-access" institutions play a critical role in our unequal society. They are important gateways not only to economic success but also to richer public and personal lives for their students. Beyond the social and economic benefits to individuals, these institutions and their graduates are vital both to the nation's economic prosperity and to its cultural and human development. For all these reasons the inadequate funding of broad-access colleges is a major national problem. These institutions must have adequate resources and use them to serve their students well. Colleges—whether public, private, or for-profit—where most students fail to achieve their goals are doing more harm than good, both to their students and to the larger public that contributes to their support.

Reducing the per-student funding gaps between the selective public institutions that on the whole serve more affluent students and those that disproportionately serve first-generation students, low-income students, and students from underrepresented groups should be a national priority, in addition to being high on the agendas of all states. This need not be a zero-sum game, taking money away from more selective institutions and allocating it to broad-access colleges. Pursuing movement toward a more equal society is going to require greater investment in education at all levels; that is an effort that will have to be financed by some combination of higher taxes on those who can afford to pay and lower spending on lesser government priorities. There is no reason to think that the best place to get that money is diminished spending on public research universities, which perform many valuable economic and social roles.

It is important to remember that spending more on education is an investment that pays off in economic terms, as well as in broader social benefits, over the longer run. Government investment in education, notably including the education of disadvantaged college students, has some significant similarities to investment in physical infrastructure like roads and highways.[37] In both kinds of investment, an intensive commitment at a certain point in time yields benefits that last for decades.

It is common to suppose that the best way to get an economic payoff from educational investments is to make the education narrowly vocational. There is good reason to think, though, that this is not the way things work in an advanced economy. Even in narrow, job security terms, learning how to do a particular technical job may be imprudent, simply because rapid changes in technology may quickly render the particular skills mastered obsolete. Education of lasting vocational value should include learning how to learn new things, how to cope with uncertainty, think independently, identify and solve problems, and communicate well.

These qualities are among the ones we would like to see in our nation's citizens, along with education on the basic institutions of our democracy, a need our recent national experience surely shows. Cultivation of these qualities should in our view be designed into the curriculum and instructional practice of both two-year and four-year institutions. It definitely should

37. Koropeckyj, Lafakis, and Ozimek, "The Economic Impact of Increasing College Completion."

not be seen as a kind of education reserved for "elites." Ongoing work at the University of Wisconsin-Madison and elsewhere on how to increase the amount and the quality of effective discussion, including discussion of controversial political issues, provides insights into how to make progress in this area.[38]

Financing long-run investments for programmatic support of community colleges and broad-access universities is a complicated issue, which we will not try to resolve here in detail. The idea of a federal program with matching requirements for participating states is gaining considerable attention, with a range of proposals in Congress and from past presidential candidates. This is a promising strategy but getting the details right is a challenge.[39] Policies must provide additional funding allowing institutions to innovate and to support students as well as incentives for institutions to find more effective strategies for using whatever resources are currently available. The federal government can provide additional resources, structure incentives, and disseminate information and guidance. But state governments hold the purse strings that have the most influence over the allocation of resources across public higher education institutions. This is why a partnership is essential.

There is wide variation across apparently similar colleges with similar student bodies in how successful they are in educating undergraduates. A federal-state partnership program should have a performance floor for institutional eligibility as well as significant incentives for improvement.

The federal matching effort we envision should direct resources toward broad-access public institutions and the students

38. See the website of the University of Wisconsin School of Education Discussion Project for more information.

39. Baum and McPherson, *Strengthening the Federal Role in the Federal-State Partnership for Funding Higher Education.*

they serve. These investments should have the effect of reducing the gaps in per-student spending at more and less selective institutions. But, given the importance of well-designed educational investments in reducing inequality, this gap-closing should take the form of leveling up rather than leveling down.

The federal government needs to do more than simply count on individual administrators to follow the widely publicized examples of Georgia State, Florida State, CUNY ASAP, and others that have made impressive strides in student outcomes, as we recommended in the previous chapter. We need a funding program accompanied by a systematic national effort to disseminate information about best practices for supporting at-risk students and to provide strong incentives for institutions to implement these practices. Competitive grant programs, facilitated interactions, and well-designed rewards for successful implementation of support systems that work for students all have the potential to influence institutional priorities and practices.

Recommendations

We need to develop a well-designed federal-state partnership to create stronger incentives for states to fund higher education adequately and equitably. This will involve strategies for narrowing the gaps in the opportunities offered across states, as well as the gaps in per-student funding across institutions within states.

Holding Institutions Accountable for Student Outcomes

Both federal and state governments have a role to play in holding postsecondary institutions accountable for student outcomes. About two-thirds of states have implemented funding systems that base appropriations at least partly on factors such as time to degree, graduation and retention rates, and enroll-ment and success of low-income students.[40] The evidence of the effectiveness of elaborate versions of so-called "performance-based funding" policies is not yet convincing, but providing incentives beyond just enrolling more students is clearly ap-propriate. However, performance-based funding will not solve all of the problems in this area. For example, decreasing funding for institutions whose performance is already undermined by resource constraints is unlikely to solve the problems facing at-risk students. Creative thinking at the state level—and in many cases additional resources—will be required to align resources with student needs.

The federal government, which provides more than $150 bil-lion a year to students in all sectors of higher education in the form of grants, loans, and tax credits, also has a responsibility to hold institutions accountable for outcomes. Most ideas for federal accountability strategies involve monitoring student borrowing and loan repayment.[41] The Gainful Employment rule, designed by the Obama administration and repealed by the Trump administration, would have excluded for-profit pro-grams and non-degree programs at other institutions from par-ticipating in federal student aid programs if their graduates had very high debt levels relative to their earnings and low repay-ment rates. A number of proposals suggest charging institutions for a share of the loans on which their students default. It is not easy to design accountability systems that avoid counterpro-ductive consequences at the same time that they effectively improve institutional quality. But it is surely possible, and the

40. HCM Strategists, "Outcomes-Based Funding."
41. For a well-thought-out proposal, see Looney and Watson, "A Risk-Sharing Proposal to Hold Higher Ed Institutions Accountable to Their Students."

federal government cannot continue to fund students to enroll in institutions and programs unlikely to serve them well, frequently leaving them with debt and no degree.

A central challenge in developing outcomes standards is how to account for differences in incoming students. No institutional magic will allow students who entered college with limited skills and knowledge to emerge indistinguishable from those whose earlier life experiences prepared them well for any academic challenge. Comparing institutions without accounting for these differences is counterproductive. On the other hand, setting low expectations for students who start college less prepared can doom them to poor outcomes.

Recommendations

Both state and federal governments have roles to play in ensuring that colleges and universities provide high-quality educational opportunities to their students. States should ensure that institutions face appropriate incentives (by, for example, rewarding them for graduating low-income students with degrees of value) and have the resources to meet their goals. The federal government should have strict standards that prevent students from using their federal financial aid at programs and institutions that are unlikely to serve them well. Setting moderate thresholds for completion rates, post-college employment and earnings, and debt repayment that apply to all institutions, regardless of their student bodies, has the potential to steer students away from schools likely to do them damage without setting targets that are impossible for open-access institutions to meet.

Accountability must pay special attention to for-profit institutions. There are high-quality and low-quality institutions in all sectors, but there is a clear pattern of more frequent fraud and abuse, unacceptably high levels of student borrowing and default, and low degree-completion rates in the for-profit sector. Regulations must be strong enough to prevent institutions from making false promises and leaving students worse off than they would be if they had not enrolled in college at all. The Gainful Employment rule was far from perfect but provides a good starting point for rebuilding an effective regulatory system.

Sustaining a Focus on Quality

It is important to qualify the goal of increasing the share of adults with college degrees by emphasizing the importance of quality. If we redefine bachelor's and/or associate degrees by diminishing the learning required for people to earn these credentials, they are likely to become less valuable in contributing to students' personal growth and workplace productivity. Just handing out pieces of paper might temporarily change the balance in the labor market but would almost certainly increase the demand for other, more meaningful, credentials. It might, for example, accelerate the increase in the share of college graduates who are good students going on to graduate school— and the share of employers who demand advanced degrees.

As we observed earlier and as leading economists also argue,[42] the payoff to college does not come mainly from acquiring specific vocational skills but rather from developing skills and habits of mind that make people better communicators, problem identifiers, and problem solvers throughout their lives. It is this kind of education that allows workers to succeed in the face of rapid technical change—and that allows citizens to be sound political and civic actors in a rapidly changing world.

---

42. Deming and Kahn, "Skill Requirements across Firms and Labor Markets"; Deming, "The Growing Importance of Social Skills in the Labor Market."

Some of the approaches discussed in the preceding chapter, including improved approaches to developmental education, intrusive advising, and guided pathways, hold promise for improving both completion rates and the quality of the educational experience. A key factor in focusing on quality is ensuring that all of the attention does not go either to the prices students pay or to the number of students completing credentials, important as those issues are. Rather, the question should always be whether students are learning and acquiring skills and perspectives that will serve them well throughout their lives.

Recommendations

Quality and learning are more difficult to measure than prices, completion rates, and debt repayment. But we must keep quality and learning at the top of the list of goals for postsecondary education. Both federal and state governments should provide incentives and support for improved student learning. One route to doing so might be a competitive grant program for experimental efforts to improve teaching.

The federal government should also support advising in the choice of what institution to attend and what program to enroll in at the institution attended. The government already makes available a "College Scorecard" website that provides information on prices, financial aid, and graduation rate, as well as other data, for individual colleges. But making such information available only passively is not enough to get students to seek it out and use it well. The government should support programs that train high school counselors in advising students about their college choices and should provide robust programs in the military to educate soldiers and sailors leaving the military about their educational and training options.

Too often, the principal source of advice for students choosing a college is provided by the college they wind up attending. Such advice is often neither reliable nor objective, perhaps especially in the case of for-profit institutions. We continue to support a recommendation from a panel we served on some years ago that the federal government should operate advising centers where all students seeking Pell Grants would be required to participate in an advising session.[43]

Students need advice not only about what school to attend but also about what program makes sense for them. In a four-year college, this may be choice of major; in a two-year or shorter program it may be that, or it may be a pre-professional program in, say, computer technology or HVAC.

Too much of the available information and guidance students receive about program choice is tied directly to average earnings of graduates. (Median earnings two years after graduation is the only "outcome" measure reported on the College Scorecard website, and it includes only students who received federal financial aid.) For one thing, relative wages across majors or programs fluctuate over time. Also, the average earnings in a particular occupation aren't a good predictor of what any individual will earn. More important, earnings are far from the be-all and end-all of what should guide choice of institution or major or program. What choice will best prepare you to wind up with an occupation and eventually a life's work that will bring you satisfaction? We want to encourage people entering a college or vocational program to think carefully about choosing in those terms, not just provide them with misleadingly precise information about what they might earn—if they complete the program.

43. See Rethinking Pell Grants Study Group, *Rethinking Pell Grants*.

Fostering Constructive Alternatives to College

The fact that so many students enroll in college—seeking certificates, associate degrees, or bachelor's degrees—and never complete their programs contributes significantly to the reality that going to college is not always a ticket to success. As the discussion in chapter 6 emphasizes, colleges can do a lot to mitigate this problem. That said, many of these students enroll because they see no other viable option for achieving a reasonable standard of living—not because they are eager to continue their academic careers.

We should not take it as a given that enrolling in a postsecondary institution is the only way to avoid permanent financial struggles. These institutions do much more than prepare students for bachelor's degrees—many specialize in preparation for specific occupations, including those that require relatively short-term training. But there is a real question about whether the classroom is the right option for everyone seeking to improve their skills. A combination of stronger career and technical education (CTE) in high school, more apprenticeship opportunities, and other forms of on-the-job training could make it possible for alternative pathways to lead to financially remunerative and satisfying careers.

College should not be the only option.

Recommendations

In addition to removing barriers to college access and success, public policy should open other pathways. We should devote resources to evidence-based improvement in high school CTE, apprenticeships, and on-the-job training for workers with low skill levels. College should be an option for all—not a requirement to succeed in the job market. Prospective students should be made aware of these options no later than high school.

Numerous other federal and state policies could increase higher education's effectiveness in creating meaningful opportunities for students from low- and moderate-income backgrounds and from underrepresented racial and ethnic groups. No policy will work miracles. Only a combination of well-reasoned, equitable approaches will build the necessary framework for supporting a higher education system that serves the nation well.

Final Thoughts on Higher Education Policy

We want once more to remind our readers of the severe constraints that pre-college inequalities impose on colleges' ability to act and on the effectiveness of government efforts to strengthen higher education's role in increasing mobility and reducing inequality. The potential for higher education alone to narrow the social and economic inequalities in our society and to create meaningful opportunities for those who start out at the bottom to rise relative to others is heavily constrained by the extent of the structural inequalities facing people throughout their lives.

Of critical importance for policy discussions, the prices students pay for college can certainly put roadblocks on the path to economic mobility. But no reduction in tuition prices will compensate for the role of financial constraints in the pre-college years. If families cannot provide environments for their children that facilitate and nurture personal, social, intellectual, and academic development, those children will be ill-prepared to make the most of college opportunities. We must fight for more than superficial solutions.

Effective efforts to strengthen higher education's contribution to increasing opportunity, promoting social mobility, and reducing inequality will not focus narrowly on the policies and practices of selective colleges and universities, or even exclusively on reforms within higher education. Rather, they will improve the environments in which children grow up and ensure that all students have K–12 experiences that prepare them for productive lives and for further education. Public policy will support labor market structures that increase the earnings and bargaining power of low- and middle-skill workers, tax systems that generate the revenues needed to provide for good schooling and health care, a strong safety net, and opportunities for greater mobility for workers. At the broadest level, the nation's tax and transfer systems will be recalibrated in a way that promotes more equality, rather than more inequality, for the starting point of the next generation. Only if children start out in less dramatically divergent environments will it be realistic for higher education to accomplish the goals we all share.

CHAPTER 8
Conclusion

American society is too unequal in income and wealth and too limited in the degree of equality of educational and economic opportunity it affords. This book addresses the question of what we collectively can do about this and, in particular, how higher education can play a more constructive role. Our perspective is intergenerational. We have explored how our society can move deliberately—year by year, decade by decade—in the directions of less inequality in wealth and income and of more widely shared economic and educational opportunity. A major theme for us is that serious and sustained progress in these directions cannot be attained by any one of our major social institutions—not higher education, but also not preschool, not health care, and not the welfare state—acting alone.

We need a coordinated set of actions and policy changes across society if we are to move toward greater equality. To be clear, we do not envision some kind of central planning bureaucracy; instead, our vision is of a number of actors in a variety of settings all pulling in the same direction. Higher education has an important role to play and both individual institutions and public policies can and should do more even in the current context. But higher education's effectiveness is limited by dramatic inequalities in the education of children and pre-college youth, the neighborhoods in which they grow up, and the resources to which they have access, as well as by the substantial extent to which labor markets and the tax and transfer systems are biased in favor of business and the wealthy.

Emphasizing the importance of the interaction among the institutions to which people are exposed at different stages of their lives is not about shifting responsibility away from higher education. But the reality is that education builds on itself, so that early inequalities are very difficult to overcome at older ages. As Nobel economist James Heckman puts it, "capabilities beget capabilities, skills beget skills."[1] It is unrealistic to think that colleges and universities can, in a few short years of early or later adulthood, compensate for all of the differences in experiences before students come to the door.

Investments in early education bear more fruit if they are followed up with improved elementary and secondary schooling, especially for low-income and first-generation students and those from underrepresented groups. A more nearly level playing field at the time of high school graduation will expand the opportunities for students from historically disadvantaged groups to succeed in college. We understand that realizing the full benefits of such a program of systematic improvement will take decades. We must start now. We are talking here about generational change, and we should not indulge in believing that these developmental processes can be short-circuited, allowing

1. Heckman, "Schools, Skills, and Synapses," 289.

us to produce equality in college opportunity overnight. We make this argument in chapter 4, along with supporting the case for complementing investment in schooling with attention to housing, neighborhoods, and children's health that have much to do with school success.

It's not just in the school and college years, though, where we see the impact of inequality. Related forces exert pressures on market incomes and on the extent to which public policies redistribute resources. Low rates of college degree attainment result in a relative shortage of college-educated workers and a surplus of workers with less education, keeping wage gaps higher in the United States than in many other advanced countries, as we explain in chapter 5. This downward pressure on earnings for lower-income workers is reinforced by long-term increases in the market power of business relative to labor, as manifested in low minimum wages, a large drop in union membership, and steady growth in concentration of ownership within the corporate sector. Earnings differences across occupations and skill levels are larger in the United States than in many other countries. And most advanced countries rely more on a robust system of government taxes and transfers aimed at reducing the market-generated inequalities than does the United States.

In particular, a number of countries in northern Europe do a much better job than the United States in minimizing the share of families that live in severe poverty (often defined as the share with incomes below half the poverty level). An important tool in alleviating such extreme deprivation is the use of child allowances, payments that go annually on a per-child basis to all families with children. (Some such policies are means-tested; others are universal.) This policy and related strategies are especially important in the context of children's intellectual and social development where, to return to Heckman's vital point, a good early start pays major dividends later.

Higher education is sandwiched between an increasingly unequal child development and schooling system and an employment system that is increasingly hard on workers in the bottom half of the income distribution. Are we suggesting then that in the face of severe inequality before and after college, we should just let higher education policies and institutions off the hook? Or perhaps that higher education can just blame "the other guy" until high-quality schooling becomes more widespread?

This is not our message at all. Our aim in this book is to suggest that an honest look at the forces exacerbating inequality in this country over the life cycle should leave those of us who work in higher education sobered but not discouraged. It is naive at best to believe that higher education policies can "clear the slate" of all the inequities unequal childhoods visit on those from low-income families or historically disadvantaged populations. Nor is it reasonable to think that higher education can somehow inoculate its students against the unfairness and unequal power they can expect to confront in American labor markets.

Solving problems of extreme inequality and limited mobility would be much easier if financial access to college were really the primary barrier. As we discuss in detail in chapter 7, the "free college" movement promotes the idea that if only students didn't have to pay the shockingly high tuition prices charged by so many colleges, we would be far down the road to equalizing educational opportunities and outcomes. But tuition is a small piece of the puzzle. This is not only because many low-income students already receive financial aid that covers their tuition. And it's not only that covering living expenses while studying is a major hurdle for many students whose families are not in a position to support them, although certainly that is true. Instead, the biggest financial barriers are those facing families from before the day their children are born. The resources available to families to provide healthy, enriching environments for their children are in ample supply to some and totally out of reach for others. And too often people who have grown up on the wrong side of this divide have been deprived of opportunities to acquire the academic skills and social capital needed to navigate the world of college effectively.

Colleges cannot completely overcome the challenges posed by these earlier inequalities. But they can and must do more than they do now. There is plenty of room for constructive action on the part of both individual colleges and universities and state and federal governments. We can make the most difference by improving the often very low success rates at open admissions colleges and others that enroll students without strong preparation. These are the places that students from underresourced backgrounds most often attend. As we argue in chapter 6, even with the scant resources many of these institutions have, they could in many cases do better than they do now by focusing more on program completion as a central goal and by adopting practices like predictive analytics, clear academic pathways, and intrusive advising that have been pioneered by some industry leaders. At the same time, many community colleges and broad-access public institutions simply don't have enough resources to provide a high-quality experience for their students. We report in chapter 7 evidence that relatively small increases in per-student spending can reliably achieve meaningful increases in graduation rates at broad-access institutions. Underspending on the education of these students, who have disproportionately faced unequal educational opportunities from their earliest years, is a bad way for a country as wealthy as the United States to try to economize. Moreover, equity aside, studies show that greater college success for members of these groups would more than pay for itself in greater worker productivity over time.

More selective colleges and universities also need to expand their efforts to serve more low-income students. The biggest obstacle that keeps these students out of highly selective colleges is not their high tuitions, because many such colleges have very generous financial aid. As we note in chapter 7, in reality the biggest challenges are access to preparation for college and the aspiration and confidence to apply to and enroll in selective institutions. And while there are ways to make admissions processes fairer and more responsive to variations in the backgrounds of applicants, there are also strong reasons to sustain institutions with ambitious educational goals that are suitable for well-prepared students.

That said, the fact is that significant numbers of students who could meet those standards don't even try, for a variety of reasons. Low-income and first-generation students and those from underrepresented groups may not know about the financial aid that could help them pay for college and they may not know (as affluent families surely do) that going to the "right" college makes a real difference. And they may not even know how to apply.

Quantitatively, the number of such students is not large enough to make a substantial dent in combating low college success rates for disadvantaged students overall, but it could certainly make a big difference to a lot of individual students as well as enriching living and learning opportunities for all students on these campuses.

Both colleges themselves and the governments that regulate them and help support them have plenty to do in promoting progress in making our society more equal and fairer. We know that the changes we advocate, taken one a time, are modest and incremental—raising the completion rate at a community college from 20 to 30 percent; enrolling 30 more Pell Grant students at a selective liberal arts college—but increments do add up. Many observers and critics of higher education would far prefer blockbuster answers that will transform higher education. We took a look at two of these blockbuster ideas—making public colleges tuition free and providing extensive undergraduate education as a purely online experience. In chapter 7, we reviewed the reasoning and evidence supporting these ideas as dramatic "fixes" for higher education, and we found them severely wanting. We cannot wait for a silver bullet and we should not take the easy path of advocating for such narrowly targeted policy changes. Instead, we should focus on incremental improvements in the near term, coupled with lasting systemic reform, with a strong focus on the forces shaping the lives of young children.

A Thought Experiment

Consider a simple thought experiment, projecting two futures for American education in the year 2040.

In Scenario One, higher education moves forward on the lines sketched in chapters 6 and 7 but the pre-college patterns of educational and social development in the United States remain similar to those we described in chapter 4. In this scenario, we would expect higher education to make slow and steady progress in efforts to improve the prospects for students emerging into college from disadvantaged educational and social backgrounds. Broad-access institutions would continue to get better at advising and at effective remedial or developmental education; state and federal governments would become more responsive to the need for more funding at institutions where the majority of low-income and underprepared students enroll. Meanwhile, selective colleges would hone their practices for identifying, recruiting, and supporting disadvantaged students who are prepared to succeed at these institutions.

However, with no change in the conditions under which students develop before college, the big structural inequalities that mark higher education today will likely persist. Students will be sorted as now between a relatively large group who enroll disproportionately in broad-access institutions and continue to struggle with college success, and a smaller group, disproportionately White and from affluent backgrounds, who attend highly selective institutions and have greater prospects for academic, economic, and social success.

Now consider Scenario Two, where forward movement in higher education is accompanied by sustained investment in both pre-college education, all the way back to preschool, and in the neighborhoods and social institutions where disadvantaged children live. In the near term we would expect things to proceed largely as in Scenario One, although more effective performance in high schools would begin to make a difference. But if the efforts at early education improvement are sustained through grade school and high school, we should expect the profile of students as they leave high school to become dramatically different. Far too many students with historically disadvantaged backgrounds now spend much of their time in school trying to catch up—catching up with people who had better preschool opportunities, catching up on reading proficiency if their instruction in K–3 wasn't effective, catching up on math as they bring less adequate skills from elementary school. The longer-term strategy could effectively address these issues.

With a much larger share of people emerging from high school ready for college success, broad-access colleges would be able to reduce their emphasis on remediation and pour more time and resources into more advanced instruction. More people from all backgrounds would complete their postsecondary education shortly after high school, with fewer older adults finding the need to go back to school. Highly selective colleges could expect to find a much greater diversity of qualified applicants in their pools. We should expect these changes in pre-college preparation to have substantial effects on graduation, leading to less inequality in market wages. If these changes are accompanied by the kinds of post-college reforms we describe in chapter 5, the nation will be well on its way to replacing the trend toward greater inequality and narrowed opportunity we have lived with for decades with a new trend toward expanding opportunity and greater equality in living standards—replacing a vicious circle with a virtuous one.

Now of course in reality, as opposed to in thought experiments, no reform effort moves forward as smoothly and reliably as what we have imagined. Recessions and, sadly, pandemics come and go, and are sure to interrupt even excellent plans. And policies that influence inequality will always bring controversy. But having a longer-run sense of directionality about policy, especially in recognizing that education policies at one stage of the life cycle are interdependent with those at later stages, is key to lasting change.

REFERENCES

Alesina, Alberto, Edward Glaeser, and Bruce Sacerdote. "Why Doesn't the United States Have a European-Style Welfare State?" *Brookings Papers on Economic Activity* (Fall 2001): 187–27.

Alexander, Karl, Doris Entwisle, and Linda Olson. "Lasting Consequences of the Summer Learning Gap." *American Sociological Review* 72 (April 2007): 167–80. http://www.ewa.org/sites/main/files/file-attachments/summer_learning_gap -2.pdf.

Alpert, William, Kenneth Couch, and Oskar Harmon. "A Randomized Assessment of Online Learning." *American Economic Review: Papers and Proceedings* 106, no. 5 (2016): 378–82.

Altonji, Joseph, and Richard Mansfield. "The Role of Family, Community, and School Characteristics in Inequality in Education and Labor-Market Outcomes." In *Whither Opportunity? Rising Inequality, Schools, and Children's Life Chances*, edited by Greg Duncan and Richard Murnane, 187–206. New York: Russell Sage Foundation and Spencer Foundation, 2011.

American Association of Community Colleges. *Fast Facts 2020*. https://www.aacc .nche.edu/research-trends/fast-facts/.

Appiah, Kwame Anthony. *The Lies That Bind: Rethinking Identity*. New York: Liveright Press, 2018.

Ashby, Cornelia. *Many Challenges Arise in Educating Students Who Change Schools Frequently*. GAO-11-40. Washington, DC: U.S. Government Accountability Office, 2010.

Atkinson, Anthony B. *Inequality: What Can Be Done?* Cambridge, MA: Harvard University Press, 2015. Kindle edition.

Attewell, Paul, and D. Lavin. *Passing the Torch: Does Higher Education for the Disadvantaged Pay Off across the Generations?* New York: Russell Sage Foundation, 2007.

Autor, David. "Skills, Education, and the Rise of Earnings Inequality among the 'Other 99 Percent.'" *Science*, May 23, 2014. http://science.sciencemag.org/content /344/6186/843.full.

Autor, David, Lawrence Katz, and Melissa Kearney. "The Polarization of the US Labor Market." *American Economic Review* 96, no. 2 (May 2006): 189–94.

Autor, David, A. Manning, and C. L. Smith. "The Contribution of the Minimum Wage to U.S. Wage Inequality over Three Decades: A Reassessment." National Bureau of Economic Research Working Paper 1653 (2010). https://economics .mit.edu/files/3279.

Azier, Anna, Janet Currie, Peter Simon, and Patrick Vivier. "Do Low Levels of Blood Lead Reduce Children's Future Test Scores?" *American Economic Journal: Applied Economics* 10, no. 1 (2018): 307–41.

Bailey, Thomas, Shanna Smith Jaggars, and Davis Jenkins. *Redesigning America's Community Colleges: A Clearer Path to Student Success*. Cambridge, MA: Harvard University Press, 2015.

Baker, Bruce, Danielle Farrie, and David Sciarra. *Is School Funding Fair? A National Report Card*. 7th ed. Education Law Center. New Brunswick, NJ: Rutgers Graduate School of Education, 2018. https://edlawcenter.org/assets/files/pdfs /publications/Is_School_Funding_Fair_7th_Editi.pdf.

Bartels, Larry, Hugh Heclo, Rodney Hero, and Lawrence Jacobs. "Inequality and American Governance." In *Inequality and American Democracy*, edited by Lawrence Jacobs and Theda Skocpol, 88–155. New York: Russell Sage Foundation, 2005.

Basch, David. "Healthier Students Are Better Learners: A Missing Link in School Reforms to Close the Achievement Gap." *Journal of School Health* 81, no. 10 (2011): 593–98.

Baum, Sandy, and Victoria Lee. *Understanding Endowments*. Washington, DC: Urban Institute, 2018. https://www.urban.org/sites/default/files/publication/98206 /understanding_endowments_1.pdf.

Baum, Sandy, and Adam Looney. "Who Owes the Most in Student Loans: New Data from the Fed." Brookings. October 9, 2020. https://www.brookings.edu/blog/up -front/2020/10/09/who-owes-the-most-in-student-loans-new-data-from-the -fed/.

Baum, Sandy, Jennifer Ma, Matea Pender, and C. J. Libassi. *Trends in Student Aid, 2018*. New York: College Board, 2018.

Baum, Sandy, and Donald Marron. "What Would Forgiving Student Debt Mean for the Federal Budget?" *Urban Wire*, December 22, 2020. https://www.urban.org /urban-wire/what-would-forgiving-student-debt-mean-federal-budget.

Baum, Sandy, and Michael McPherson. "'Free College' Does Not Eliminate Student Debt." *Urban Wire*, August 22, 2019. https://www.urban.org/urban-wire/free -college-does-not-eliminate-student-debt.

———. "Improving Teaching: Strengthening the College Learning Experience." *Daedalus, the Journal of the American Academy of Arts and Sciences* 148, no. 4 (Fall 2019): 5–13.

———. "Sorting to Extremes." *Change* 43, no. 4 (July/August 2011): 6–12.

———. *Strengthening the Federal Role in the Federal-State Partnership for Funding Higher Education.* Washington, DC: Urban Institute, December 2020.

Baum, Sandy, and Saul Schwartz. "Unaffordable Loans: When Should Schools Become Ineligible for Student Loan Programs?" Washington, DC: Urban Institute, 2018. https://www.urban.org/research/publication/unaffordable-loans-when -should-schools-become-ineligible-student-loan-programs.

Baum, Sandy, and Judith Scott-Clayton. *Redesigning the Pell Grant Program for the Twenty-First Century.* Washington, DC: Hamilton Project, 2013.

Bayer, Patrick, and Kerwin Kofi Charles. "Divergent Paths: A New Perspective on Earnings Differences between Black and White Men since 1940." *Quarterly Journal of Economics* (August 2018): 1459–1501.

Becker, Gary. *Human Capital.* New York: Columbia University Press, 1964.

Berg, Janine. "Labour Market Institutions: The Building Blocks of Just Societies." In *Labour Markets, Institutions and Inequality Building Just Societies in the 21st Century,* edited by Janine Berg, 1–36. Northampton, MA: Edward Elgar, 2015.

Bettinger, Eric, and Rachel Baker. "The Effects of Student Coaching: An Evaluation of a Randomized Experiment in Student Advising." *Educational Evaluation and Policy Analysis* 36, no. 1 (2014): 3–19.

Bettinger, Eric, and Susanna Loeb. "Promises and Pitfalls of Online Education." *Evidence Speaks.* Brookings, 2017. https://www.brookings.edu/wp-content/uploads /2017/06/ccf_20170609_loeb_evidence_speaks1.pdf.

Black, Dan, and Jeffrey Smith. "Estimating the Returns to College Quality with Multiple Proxies for Quality." *Journal of Labor Economics* 24, no. 3 (2006): 701–28.

———. "How Robust Is the Evidence on the Effects of College Quality? Evidence from Matching." *Journal of Econometrics* 121 (2004): 99–124.

Black, Sandra E., Jeffrey T. Denning, and Jesse Rothstein. "Winners and Losers? The Effect of Gaining and Losing Access to Selective Colleges on Education and Labor Market Outcomes." National Bureau of Economic Research. 2020. http:// www.nber.org/papers/w26821.

Bowen, William, Matthew Chingos, Kelly Lack, and Thomas Nygren. "Interactive Learning Online at Public Universities: Evidence from a Six-Campus Randomized Trial." *Journal of Policy Analysis and Management* 33, no. 1 (2014): 94–111.

Bowen, William, Matthew Chingos, and Michael McPherson. "Helping Students Finish the 4-Year Run." *Chronicle of Higher Education,* September 8, 2009.

Bowen, William, Martin Kurzweil, and Eugene Tobin. *Equity and Excellence in American Higher Education.* Charlottesville: University of Virginia Press, 2005.

Brand, J., and Y. Xie. "Who Benefits Most from College? Evidence for Negative Selection in Heterogeneous Economic Returns to Higher Education." *American Sociological Review* 75 (2010): 273–302.

Brennan, Maya. *The Positive Impacts of Affordable Housing on Education: A Research Summary.* Center for Housing Policy, 2007. https://www.enterprisecommunity.org/download?fid=8082&nid=4636.

Brighouse, Harry. "Ethical Leadership in Hard Times: The Moral Demands on Universities." *Forum Futures* (2010): 51–56. http://forum.mit.edu/wp-content/uploads/2017/05/FF10EthicalLdrspHardTimes.pdf.

British Broadcasting Company. "What Remote Jobs Tell Us about Inequality." September 21, 2020. https://www.bbc.com/worklife/article/20200921-what-remote-jobs-tell-us-about-inequality.

Bruni, Frank. "How to Survive the College Admissions Madness." *New York Times,* March 15, 2014. https://www.nytimes.com/2015/03/15/opinion/sunday/frank-bruni-how-to-survive-the-college-admissions-madness.html?_r=1.

Burdick-Will, Julia, Jens Ludwig, Stephen Raudenbush, Robert Sampson, Lisa Sanbonmatsu, and Patrick Sharkey. "Converging Evidence for Neighborhood Effects on Children's Test Scores: An Experimental, Quasi-Experimental, and Observational Comparison." In *Whither Opportunity? Rising Inequality, Schools, and Children's Life Chances,* edited by Greg Duncan and Richard Murnane, 255–76. New York: Russell Sage Foundation and Spencer Foundation, 2011.

Burkam, David, Valerie Lee, and Julie Dwyer. "School Mobility in the Early Elementary Grades: Frequency and Impact from Nationally-Representative Data." In *Student Mobility: Exploring the Impact of Frequent Moves on Achievement,* National Research Council and Institute of Medicine. Washington, DC: National Academies Press, 2010. https://doi.org/10.17226/12853.

Burke, Lilah. "Assessing the Value of an Undergrad Degree." *Inside Higher Education,* September 27, 2019.

Campus Compact. https://compact.org/.

Card, David. "Estimating the Return to Schooling: Progress on Some Persistent Econometric Problems." *Econometrica* 69 (September 2001): 1127–1360.

Carneiro, Pedro, and James J. Heckman. "The Evidence on Credit Constraints in Post-Secondary Schooling." *Economic Journal* 112 (October 2002): 705–34.

Carolina Abecedarian Project. "Scholarly Publications." https://abc.fpg.unc.edu/summaries-and-stories.

Carrell, Scott, Mark Hoekstra, and Elira Kuka. "The Long-Run Effects of Disruptive Peers." *American Economic Review* 108, no. 11 (2018): 3377–3415.

Carroll, Aaron. "Preventive Care Saves Money? Sorry, It's Too Good to Be True." *New York Times,* January 29, 2018.

Center for Community College Student Engagement. *Show Me the Way: The Power of Advising in Community Colleges.* 2018 National Report. Austin, TX: CCCSE, 2018.

Chakrabarti, Rajashri, and Michelle Jiang. "Education's Role in Earnings, Employment, and Economic Mobility." *Liberty Street Economics.* Federal Reserve Bank of New York, 2018. https://libertystreeteconomics.newyorkfed.org/2018/09/educations-role-in-earnings-employment-and-economic-mobility.html.

Chetty, Raj, John Friedman, Emmanuel Saez, Nicholas Turner, and Danny Yagan. "The Determinants of Income Segregation and Intergenerational Mobility Using Test Scores to Measure Undermatching." National Bureau of Economic Research Working Paper. 2020. Opportunity Insights. https://opportunityinsights.org/wp-content/uploads/2020/02/coll_mrc_NBER_paper.pdf.

Chetty, Raj, David Grusky, Maximilian Hell, Nathaniel Hendren, Robert Manduca, and Jimmy Narang. "The Fading American Dream: Trends in Absolute Income Mobility since 1940." *Science* 356 (2017): 398–406.

Chetty, Raj, and Nathaniel Hendren. "The Impacts of Neighborhoods on Intergenerational Mobility I: Childhood Exposure Effects." *Quarterly Journal of Economics* 113, no. 3 (2018): 1107–62.

Chetty, Raj, Nathaniel Hendren, and Lawrence Katz. "The Effects of Exposure to Better Neighborhoods on Children: New Evidence from the Moving to Opportunity Project." *American Economic Review* 106, no. 4 (2016): 855–902. https://scholar.harvard.edu/files/hendren/files/mto_paper.pdf.

Chetty, Raj, Nathaniel Hendren, Patrick Kline, Emmanuel Saez, and Nicholas Turner. "Is the United States Still a Land of Opportunity? Recent Trends in Intergenerational Mobility." National Bureau of Economic Research Working Paper 19844. 2014. http://www.nber.org/papers/w19844.

Chingos, Matthew. "Who Would Benefit Most from Free College?" *Evidence Speaks.* Brookings, 2016. https://www.brookings.edu/research/who-would-benefit-most-from-free-college/.

Clark, Burton. "The 'Cooling-Out' Function in Higher Education." *American Journal of Sociology* 65, no. 6 (May 1960): 569–76.

Cohen, Robin, Emily Zammitti, and Michael Martinez. *Health Insurance Coverage: Early Release of Estimates from the National Health Interview Survey, 2017.* Washington, DC: National Center for Health Statistics, 2017. https://www.cdc.gov/nchs/data/nhis/earlyrelease/insur201805.pdf.

Cohodes, Sarah, Daniel Grossman, Samuel Kleiner, and Michael Lovenheim. "The Effect of Child Health Insurance Access on Schooling: Evidence from Public Insurance Expansions." *Journal of Human Resources* 51, no. 3 (2016): 727–59.

Coley, Rebekah, Alicia Lynch, and Melissa Kull. "The Effects of Housing and Neighborhood Chaos on Children." How Housing Matters. Chicago: MacArthur

Foundation, 2014. https://www.macfound.org/media/files/HHM_Brief_-_The _Effects_of_Housing_Neighborhood_Chaos_on_Children.pdf.

Colton, Claudia, Francisca Richter, Seok-Joo Kim, Robert Fischer, and Youngmin Cho. "Temporal Effects of Distressed Housing on Early Childhood Risk Factors and Kindergarten Readiness." *Children and Youth Services Review* 68 (September 2016): 59–72. https://www.minneapolisfed.org/~/media/files/community /2017-conference/papers-and-presentations/concurrent3/richter_paper_508 .pdf?la=en.

Community-wealth.org. Democracy Collaborative. https://community-wealth.org.

Conley, Dalton, and Neil Bennett. "Is Biology Destiny? Birth Weight and Life Chances." *American Sociological Review* 65, no. 3 (2000): 458–67.

Corak, Miles. "Do Poor Children Become Poor Adults? Lessons from a Cross Country Comparison of Generational Earnings Mobility." *Research on Economic Inequality* 13 (2006): 143–88.

———. "Income Inequality, Equality of Opportunity, and Intergenerational Mobility." *Journal of Economic Perspectives* 27, no. 3 (Summer 2013): 79–103. https://pubs .aeaweb.org/doi/pdf/10.1257/jep.27.3.79.

Cornish, Audie. "Study Finds Many Companies Require Non-Compete Clauses for Low-Wage Workers." *All Things Considered.* National Public Radio, November 7, 2016. https://www.npr.org/2016/11/07/501053238/study-finds-many -companies-require-non-compete-clauses-for-low-wage-workers.

Crowder, Kyle, and Scott J. South. "Spatial and Temporal Dimensions of Neighborhood Effects on High School Graduation." *Social Science Research* 40 (2011): 87–106.

Cuhna, Flavio, and James Heckman. "The Technology of Skill Formation." *American Economic Review* 97, no. 2 (2007): 31–47.

Dale, Stacy, and Alan Krueger. "Estimating the Payoff to Attending a More Selective College: An Application of Selection on Observables and Unobservables." *Quarterly Journal of Economics* 117, no. 4 (2002): 1491–1528.

———. "Estimating the Return to College Selectivity over the Career Using Administrative Earnings Data." *Journal of Human Resources* 49, no. 2 (Spring 2014): 323–58.

Deming, David. "Early Childhood Intervention and Life-Cycle Skill Development: Evidence from Head Start." *American Economic Journal: Applied Economics* 1, no. 3 (2009): 111–34.

———. "The Growing Importance of Social Skills in the Labor Market." *Quarterly Journal of Economics* 132, no. 4 (2017): 1593–1640.

Deming, David, Claudia Goldin, Lawrence Katz, and Noam Yuchtman. "Can Online Learning Bend the Higher Education Cost Curve?" *American Economic Review: Papers and Proceedings* 105, no. 5 (2015): 496–501.

Deming, David, and Lisa Kahn. "Skill Requirements across Firms and Labor Markets: Evidence from Job Postings for Professionals." *Journal of Labor Economics* 36, no. S1 (2018): S337–S369.

Duncan, Greg, and Katherine Magnuson. "The Nature and Impact of Early Achievement Skills, Attention Skills, and Behavior Problems." In *Whither Opportunity: Rising Inequality, Schools, and Children's Life Chances*, edited by Greg Duncan and Richard Murnane, 347–70. New York: Russell Sage Foundation and Spencer Foundation, 2011.

Duncan, Greg, and Richard Murnane. "Introduction: The American Dream Then and Now." In *Whither Opportunity: Rising Inequality, Schools, and Children's Life Chances*, edited by Greg Duncan and Richard Murnane, 3–23. New York: Russell Sage Foundation and Spencer Foundation, 2011.

———. "Rising Inequality in Family Incomes and Children's Educational Outcomes." *Russell Sage Foundation Journal of the Social Sciences* 2, no. 2 (May 2017): 42–158. https://muse.jhu.edu/article/616924/pdf.

Dynarski, Susan. "Online Courses Are Harming the Students Who Need the Most Help." *New York Times*, January 19, 2018.

Escueta, Maya, Vincent Quan, Andre Joshua Nickow, and Philip Oreopoulos. "Education Technology: An Evidence-Based Review." National Bureau of Economic Research Working Paper 23744. 2017.

Fallows, James, and Deborah Fallows. *Our Towns: A 100,000-Mile Journey into the Heart of America*. New York: Pantheon Books, 2018.

Farkas, George. "Middle and High School Skills Behaviors, Attitudes, Curriculum Enrollment, and Their Consequences." In *Whither Opportunity: Rising Inequality, Schools, and Children's Life Chances*, edited by Greg Duncan and Richard Murnane, 71–90. New York: Russell Sage Foundation and Spencer Foundation, 2011.

Figlio, David. "A Silver Lining for Online Higher Education?" *Brookings: Evidence Speaks*. 2016. https://www.brookings.edu/research/a-silver-lining-for-online-higher-education/.

Figlio, David, Jonathan Guryan, Krzysztof Karbownik, and Jeffrey Roth. "The Effects of Poor Neonatal Health on Children's Cognitive Development." *American Economic Review* 104, no. 12 (2014): 3921–55.

Figlio, David, Mark Rush, and Lu Yin. "Is It Live or Is It Internet? Experimental Estimates of the Effects of Online Instruction on Student Learning." *Journal of Labor Economics* 31, no. 4 (2013): 763–84.

Fink, John, David Jenkins, and Takeshi Yanagiura. *What Happens to Students Who Take Community College "Dual Enrollment" Courses in High School?* Community College Research Center, 2017.

Fischer, Karin. "Engine of Inequality." *Chronicle of Higher Education*, January 17, 2016. https://www.chronicle.com/article/Engine-of-Inequality/234952?cid=cp42.

———. "Tackling the Equity Challenge from All Sides." *Chronicle of Higher Education*, December 31, 2019. https://www.chronicle.com/interactives/20191231 -barriers-case-studies.

568 Presidents Group. Updated 2021. 568group.org/.

Frank, Robert. "Positional Externalities Cause Large and Preventable Welfare Losses." *American Economic Review* 95, no. 2 (2005): 137–41.

Freeman, Richard. *The Overeducated American*. Cambridge, MA: Academic Press, 1976.

Furman, Jason, and Larry Summers. "A Reconsideration of Fiscal Policy in the Era of Low Interest Rates, Discussion Draft." Brookings Institution, November 30, 2020.

Galster, George, Dave Marcotte, Marv Mandell, Hal Wolman, and Nancy Augustine. "The Influence of Neighborhood Poverty during Childhood on Fertility, Education, and Earnings Outcomes." *Housing Studies* 22, no. 5 (2007): 723–51. https:// doi.org/10.1080/02673030701474669.

Galster, George, et al. "Neighborhood Effects on Secondary School Performance of Latino and African American Youth: Evidence from a Natural Experiment in Denver." *Journal of Urban Economics* 93 (2016): 30–48. https://www.researchgate .net/publication/282158250_Neighborhood_Effects_on_Secondary_School _Performance_of_Latino_and_African_American_Youth_Evidence_from_a _Natural_Experiment_in_Denver.

Garces, Elianak, Duncan Thomas, and Janet Currie. "Longer Term Effects of Head Start." *American Economic Review* 92, no. 4 (2002): 999–1012.

Goldin, Claudia, and Lawrence Katz. "Long-Run Changes in the Wage Structure: Narrowing, Widening, Polarizing." *Brookings Papers on Economic Activity* 135 (Fall 2007). https://www.brookings.edu/wp-content/uploads/2007/09/2007b _bpea_goldin.pdf

———. *The Race between Education and Technology*. Cambridge, MA: Belknap Press, 2008.

Goodman, Joshua, Julia Melkers, and Amanda Pallais. "Can Online Delivery Increase Access to Education?" National Bureau of Economic Research Working Paper 22754. 2016. http://www.nber.org/papers/w22754.

Greenstone, Michael, Adam Looney, Jeremy Patashnik, and Muxin Yu. "Thirteen Economic Facts about Social Mobility and the Role of Education." Brookings Institution, 2016.

Grossman, Daniel, Samuel Kleiner, and Michael Lovenheim. "The Effect of Child Health Insurance Access on Schooling: Evidence from Public Insurance Expansions." *Journal of Human Resources* 51, no. 3 (2016): 727–59.

Hacker, Jacob. "The Institutional Foundations of Middle-Class Democracy." *Policy Network* 6 (2011): 33–37. https://www.jacobhacker.com/assets/hacker_pn.pdf.

Harding, David. "Counterfactual Models of Neighborhood Effects: The Effect of Neighborhood Poverty on Dropping Out and Teenage Pregnancy." *American Journal of Sociology* 109, no. 3 (November 2003): 676–719.

Haskins, Ron. "Education and Economic Mobility." In *Getting Ahead or Losing Ground: Economic Mobility in America*, edited by Ron Haskins, Julia Isaacs, and Isabel Sawhill. Washington, DC: Brookings Institution, 2008.

HCM Strategists. "Outcomes-Based Funding: Driving Outcomes for Students through Aligned Funding Models." 2019. http://hcmstrategists.com/how-we-do-it/case -studies/obf-driving-outcomes-for-students-through-aligned-funding-models/.

Heckman, James. "Schools, Skills, and Synapses." 2008. https://heckmanequation .org/assets/2017/01/051409_Heckman_ppt_hires.pdf.

Heckman, James, and Henry Schultz. "Invest in the Very Young." *Encyclopedia on Early Childhood Development*. 2017. http://www.child-encyclopedia.com/sites /default/files/textes-experts/en/669/invest-in-the-very-young.pdf.

Hernandez, Donald. *Double Jeopardy: How Third-Grade Reading Skills and Poverty Influence High School Graduation*. Baltimore: Annie E. Casey Foundation, April 2011. https://files.eric.ed.gov/fulltext/ED518818.pdf.

Hertz, Tom. *Understanding Mobility in America*. Washington, DC: Center for American Progress, 2006.

Hess, Frederick, and Joseph Fuller. "The Pay-off for a Prestigious College Degree Is Smaller than You Think." *The Hill*, June 2, 2020.

Hill, Catharine. "American Higher Education and Income Inequality." *Education Finance and Policy* 11, no. 3 (2016): 325–39. https://www.mitpressjournals.org/doi /abs/10.1162/EDFP_a_00178?journalCode=edfp.

Hoekstra, Mark. "The Effect of Attending the Flagship State University on Earnings: A Discontinuity-Based Approach." *Review of Economics and Statistics* 91, no. 4 (2009): 717–72.

Hoxby, Caroline. "The Changing Selectivity of American Colleges." *Journal of Economic Perspectives* 23, no. 4 (2009): 95–118.

Hoxby, Caroline, and Christopher Avery. "The Missing 'One-Offs': The Hidden Supply of High-Achieving, Low-Income Students." *Brookings Papers on Economic Activity* (Spring 2013): 1–50.

International Labor Organization. "Industrial Relations." ILOSTAT. 2019. http:// www.ilo.org/ilostat/.

Ip, Greg. "Is Elite College Worth It? Maybe Not." *Wall Street Journal*, March 20, 2019.

Isaacs, Julia, and Isabel Sawhill. "Reaching for the Prize: The Limits on Economic Mobility." Brookings Institution, 2008.

Jacobs, Lawrence, and Theda Skocpol, eds. *Inequality and American Democracy: What We Know and What We Need to Learn*. New York: Russell Sage Foundation, 2005. www.jstor.org/stable/10.7758/9781610443043.

Jäntti, Markus, Brent Bratsberg, Knut Roed, and Oddbjörn Rauum. "American Exceptionalism in a New Light: A Comparison of Intergenerational Earnings Mobility in the Nordic Countries, the United Kingdom and the United States." IZA Discussion Paper No. 1938. Bonn: Institute for the Study of Labor, 2010.

Jargowsky, Paul. *The Architecture of Segregation: Civil Unrest, the Concentration of Poverty, and Public Policy*. New York: The Century Foundation, 2015. https://s3-us-west-2.amazonaws.com/production.tcf.org/app/uploads/2015/08/07182514/Jargowsky_ArchitectureofSegregation-11.pdf.

Johnson, Lyndon. "Remarks at Southwest Texas State College upon Signing the Higher Education Act of 1965." *American Presidency Project*, 1965. https://www.presidency.ucsb.edu/documents/remarks-southwest-texas-state-college-upon-signing-the-higher-education-act-1965.

Joint Center for Housing Studies of Harvard University. *The State of the Nation's Housing, 2018*. Cambridge, MA: Harvard University, 2018. http://www.jchs.harvard.edu/sites/default/files/Harvard_JCHS_State_of_the_Nations_Housing_2018.pdf.

Jyoti, Diana, Edward Frongilio, and Sonya Jones. "Food Insecurity Affects School Children's Academic Performance, Weight Gain, and Social Skills." *Journal of Nutrition* 135, no. 12 (2005): 2831–39.

Kaushal, Neeraj, Katherine Magnuson, and Jane Waldfogel. "How Is Family Income Related to Investments in Children's Learning?" In *Whither Opportunity? Rising Inequality, Schools, and Children's Life Chances*, edited by Greg Duncan and Richard Murnane, 187–206. New York: Russell Sage Foundation and Spencer Foundation, 2011.

Kent, Ana, and Lowell Ricketts. "What Wealth Inequality in America Looks Like: Key Facts & Figures." *Open Vault Blog*. Federal Reserve Bank of St. Louis, August 14, 2019. https://www.stlouisfed.org/open-vault/2019/august/wealth-inequality-in-america-facts-figures.

Kerbow, David, Carlos Azcoitia, and Barbara Buell. "Student Mobility and Local School Improvement in Chicago." *Journal of Negro Education* 72, no. 1 (2003): 158–64.

King, Martin Luther Jr. "The American Dream" sermon. 1965. https://kinginstitute.stanford.edu/king-papers/documents/american-dream-sermon-delivered-ebenezer-baptist-church.

Kingsley, G. Thomas. *Trends in Housing Problems and Federal Housing Assistance*. Washington, DC: Urban Institute, 2017. https://www.urban.org/sites/default/files/publication/94146/trends-in-housing-problems-and-federal-housing-assistance.pdf.

Koropeckyj, Sophia, Chris Lafakis, and Adam Ozimek. "The Economic Impact of Increasing College Completion." Research Paper. American Academy of Arts and Sciences, 2017.

Krueger, Alan. "The Rise and Consequences of Inequality in the United States." 2012. https://milescorak.files.wordpress.com/2012/01/34af5d01.pdf.

Krugman, Paul. "The Great Gatsby Curve." *New York Times*, January 15, 2012.

Lacour, Misty, and Laura Tissington. "The Effects of Poverty on Academic Achievement." *Educational Research and Reviews* 6, no. 7 (2011): 522–27.

Ladd, Abigail. "Education and Poverty: Confronting the Evidence." Presidential Address. *Journal of Policy Analysis and Management* 31, no. 2 (2012): 203–27.

Lareau, Annette. *Unequal Childhoods*. Berkeley: University of California Press, 2003.

Le, Cindy, Elizabeth Davidson Pisacreta, James Dean Ward, and Jesse Margolis. *Expanding Pathways to College Enrollment and Degree Attainment: Policies and Reforms for a Diverse Population*. New York: Ithaka S&R, 2019. https://doi.org/10.18665/sr.312296.

Lemieux, Thomas. "Postsecondary Education and Increasing Wage Inequality." *American Economic Review* 96, no. 2 (May 2006): 195–99.

Leventhal, Tama, and Jeanne Brooks-Gunn. "A Randomized Study of Neighborhood Effects on Low-Income Children's Educational Outcomes." *Developmental Psychology* 40, no. 4 (2004): 488–50.

Levine, Phillip, and Diane Schanzenbach. "The Impact of Children's Public Health Insurance Expansions on Educational Outcomes." *Forum for Health Economics and Policy* 12, no. 1 (2009): 1–28.

Long, Mark. "Changes in the Returns to Education and College Quality." *Economics of Education Review* 29, no. 3 (2010): 338–47.

———. "College Quality and Early Adult Outcomes." *Economics of Education Review* 27, no. 5 (2008): 588–602.

Looney, Adam, and Tara Watson. "A Risk-Sharing Proposal to Hold Higher Ed Institutions Accountable to Their Students." Washington, DC: Brookings, 2018. https://www.brookings.edu/research/a-risk-sharing-proposal-to-hold-higher-ed-institutions-accountable-to-their-students/.

Ludwig, Jens, and Douglass Miller. "Does Head Start Improve Children's Life Chances? Evidence from a Regression Discontinuity Design." *Quarterly Journal of Economics* 122, no. 1 (2007): 159–208.

Ma, Jennifer, Sandy Baum, Matea Pender, and C. J. Libassi. *Trends in College Pricing, 2018*. New York: College Board, 2018.

———. *Trends in College Pricing, 2019*. New York: College Board, 2019.

Ma, Jennifer, Matea Pender, and C. J. Libassi. *Trends in College Pricing, 2020*. College Board, 2020. trends.collegeboard.org.

Marcotte, David. "Something in the Air? Air Quality and Children's Educational Outcomes." *Economics of Education Review* 56 (2017): 141–51.

Markovits, Daniel. *The Meritocracy Trap: How America's Foundational Myth Feeds Inequality, Dismantles the Middle Class, and Devours the Elite.* New York: Penguin Press, 2019.

Marmot, Michael. *Status Syndrome: How Your Place on the Social Gradient Directly Affects Your Health.* London: Bloomsbury, 2015.

Masten, Ann, Arturo Sesma, Rekhhet Si-Asar, Catherine Lawrence, Donna Miliotis, and Jacqueline Dionne. "Educational Risks for Children Experiencing Homelessness." *Journal of Social Psychology* 35, no. 1 (1997): 27–46.

McPherson, Michael, and Lawrence Bacow. "Online Higher Education: Beyond the Hype Cycle." *Journal of Economic Perspectives* 29, no. 4 (2015): 135–53.

Mettler, Suzanne. "How U.S. Higher Education Promotes Inequality—and What Can Be Done to Broaden Access and Graduation." *Scholars Strategy Network,* October 1, 2014. https://scholars.org/brief/how-us-higher-education-promotes-inequality-%E2%80%93-and-what-can-be-done-broaden-access-and.

Mueller, Elizabeth, and Rosie Tighe. "Making the Case for Affordable Housing: Connecting Housing with Health and Education." *Journal of Planning Literature* 24, no. 4 (April 2007): 371.

Mueller, Tom, Kathryn McConnell, Paul Berne Burow, Katie Pofahl, Alexis A. Merdjanoff, and Justin Farrell. "Impacts of the COVID-19 Pandemic on Rural America." *Proceedings of the National Academy of Sciences* 118, no. 1 (January 5, 2021).

Mullainathan, Sendhil. "To Help Tackle Inequality, Remember the Advantages You've Had." The Upshot, *New York Times,* April 28, 2017. https://www.nytimes.com/2017/04/28/upshot/income-equality-isnt-just-about-headwinds-tailwinds-count-too.html.

National Academies of Sciences, Engineering, and Medicine. *A Roadmap to Reducing Child Poverty.* Edited by Greg Duncan and Suzanne Le Menestrel. Washington, DC: National Academies Press, 2019. https://doi.org/10.17226/25246.

National Association of State Student Grant and Aid Programs. *49th Annual Survey Report on State-Sponsored Student Financial Aid 2017–2018 Academic Year.* 2019. https://www.nassgapsurvey.com/survey_reports/2017-2018-49th.pdf.

National Center for Health Statistics. *Untreated Dental Caries, by Selected Characteristics.* 2017. https://www.cdc.gov/nchs/data/hus/2017/060.pdf.

National Conference of State Legislatures. "State Minimum Wages: 2019 Minimum Wage by State." http://www.ncsl.org/research/labor-and-employment/state-minimum-wage-chart.aspx.

Nelson, Charles, and Margaret Sheridan. "Lessons from Neuroscience Research for Understanding Causals Links between Family and Neighborhood Characteristics and Educational Outcomes." In *Whither Opportunity: Rising Inequality, Schools, and Children's Life Chances,* edited by Greg Duncan and Richard

Murnane, 27–46. New York: Russell Sage Foundation and Spencer Foundation, 2011.

New Haven Promise. "New Haven Promise: Making the Promise of College and Career a Reality." 2019. http://newhavenpromise.org/.

OECD. *Data: Education Spending.* 2020. https://data.oecd.org/eduresource /education-spending.htm#indicator-chart.

———. "Education and Earnings." *OECD.stat.* 2020. https://stats.oecd.org/Index .aspx?DataSetCode=EAG_EARNINGS.

———. *Government at a Glance, 2019.*

———. "Key Indicators on the Distribution of Household Disposable Income and Poverty, 2007, 2016 and 2017 or Most Recent Year." 2020. http://www.oecd.org /social/income-distribution-database.htm.

Office of Management and Budget. "Tax Expenditures." *Analytical Perspectives.* 2020.

Okun, Arthur. *Equality and Efficiency: The Big Tradeoff.* Washington, DC: Brookings Institution, 1975.

O'Neill, Martin. "Power, Predistribution, and Social Justice." *Philosophy* 95, no. 1 (January 2020): 63–91.

Oreopoulos, Philip, and Uros Petronijevic. "Making College Worth It: A Review of the Return to Higher Education." *The Future of Children* 23, no. 1 (2013): 41–65.

Oreopoulos, Philip, Mark Stabile, Randy Walld, and Leslie Roos. "The Short-, Medium-, and Long-Term Consequences of Poor Infant Health." *Journal of Human Resources* 43, no. 1 (2008): 88–138.

Pardos, Zachary A., Hung Chau, and Haocheng Zhao. "Data-Assistive Course-to-Course Articulation Using Machine Translation." Association for Computing Machinery, 2019.

Parolin, Zachary, and Emma Lee. "Large Socio-economic, Geographic, and Demographic Disparities Exist in Exposure to School Closures." *Nature Human Behaviour* 5 (2021): 522–28.

Pence, Mike. Turning Point USA. Speech. December 22, 2020. https://www.rev.com /blog/transcripts/mike-pence-speech-at-turning-point-usa-event-transcript -december-22.

Philippon, Thomas. *The Great Reversal: How America Gave Up on Free Markets.* Cambridge, MA: Harvard University Press, 2019.

Phillips, Meredith. "Parenting, Time Use, and Disparities in Academic Outcomes." In *Whither Opportunity: Growing Inequality, Schools, and Children's Life Chances,* edited by Greg J. Duncan and Richard J. Murnane. New York: Russell Sage Foundation and Spencer Foundation, 2011.

Pulliam, Christopher, and Richard Reeves. "New Child Tax Credit Could Slash Poverty Now and Boost Social Mobility Later." Brookings Middle Class Memos, March 2021.

Rasmussen, Daniel "The Gospel According to Michael Porter." *Institutional Investor*, November 7, 2019.

Raudenbush, Steven, Marshall Jean, and Emily Art. "Year-by-Year and Cumulative Impacts of Attending a High-Mobility Elementary School on Children's Mathematics Achievement in Chicago, 1995 to 2005." In *Whither Opportunity: Rising Inequality, Schools, and Children's Life Chances*, edited by Greg J. Duncan and Richard J. Murnane, 359–75. New York: Russell Sage Foundation and Spencer Foundation, 2011.

Reardon, Sean. "The Widening Academic Achievement Gap between the Rich and the Poor: New Evidence and Possible Explanations." In *Whither Opportunity? Rising Inequality, Schools, and Children's Chances*, edited by Greg Duncan and Richard Murnane, 91–116. New York: Russell Sage Foundation and Spencer Foundation, 2011.

Rethinking Pell Grants Study Group. *Rethinking Pell Grants*. New York: College Board. 2013.

Reyes, Jessica. "Lead Policy and Academic Performance: Insights from Massachusetts." *Harvard Educational Review* 85, no. 1 (2015): 75–107.

Roderick, Melissa, Matthew Holsapple, Kallie Clark, and Thomas Kelley-Kemple. *From High School to the Future: Delivering on the Dream of College Graduation*. University of Chicago Consortium on School Research, 2018.

Romney, Mitt. *Family Security Act*. https://www.romney.senate.gov/sites/default/files/2021-02/family%20security%20act_one%20pager.pdf.

Rosenbaum, James. "Changing the Geography of Opportunity by Expanding Residential Choice: Lessons from the Gautreaux Program." *Housing Policy Debate* 6, no. 1 (1995): 231–69.

Roy, Joydeep, Melissa Maynard, and Elaine Weiss. *The Hidden Costs of the Housing Crisis: The Long-Term Impact of Housing Affordability and Quality on Young Children's Odds of Success*. Partnership for America's Economic Success, 2008. https://www.pewtrusts.org/~/media/legacy/uploadedfiles/wwwpewtrustsorg/reports/partnership_for_americas_economic_success/paeshousingreportfinal1pdf.pdf.

Rutschow, Elizabeth Zachry, Maria Scott Cormier, Dominique Dukes, and Diana E. Cruz Zamora. *The Changing Landscape of Developmental Education Practices: Findings from a National Survey and Interviews with Postsecondary Institutions*. New York: MDRC, 2019.

Saez, Emmanuel, and Gabriel Zucman. *The Triumph of Injustice: How the Rich Dodge Taxes and How to Make Them Pay*. New York: W. W. Norton, 2019.

Sanbonmatsu, Lisa, Jeffrey R. Kling, Greg J. Duncan, and Jeanne Brooks-Gunn. "Neighborhoods and Academic Achievement: Results from the MTO Experiment." *Journal of Human Resources* 41, no. 4 (2006): 649–91.

Sanbonmatsu, Lisa, Jens Ludwig, Lawrence Katz, Lisa Gennetian, Greg Duncan, Ronald Kessler, Emma Adam, Thomas McDade, and Stacy Lindau. *Moving to Opportunity for Fair Housing Demonstration Program: Final Impacts Evaluation.* U.S. Department of Housing and Urban Development, 2011. https://scholar.harvard.edu/files/lkatz/files/moving_to_opportunity_for_fair_housing_demonstration_program_--_final_impacts_evaluation.pdf.

Sandel, Michael. *The Tyranny of Merit: What's Become of the Common Good?* New York: Farrar, Straus and Giroux, 2020.

Scanlon, Edward, and Kevin Devine. "Residential Mobility and Youth Well-being: Research, Policy, and Practice Issues." *Journal of Sociology and Social Welfare* 28, no. 1 (2001): 119–38.

Schaar, John. "Equality of Opportunity, and Beyond." In *Equality*, edited by Roland Pennock and John Chapman. Palo Alto: Atherton Press, 1968.

Schwartz, Heather. *Housing Policy Is School Policy: Economically Integrative Housing Promotes Academic Success in Montgomery County, MD.* New York: Century Foundation, 2010.

Scott-Clayton, Judith. "Do High-Stakes Placement Exams Predict College Success?" Community College Research Center. Working Paper No. 41. 2012.

———. "The Shapeless River: Does a Lack of Structure Inhibit Students' Progress at Community Colleges?" In *Decision Making for Student Success: Behavioral Insights to Improve College Access and Persistence*, edited by Sandy Baum, Benjamin Castleman, and Saul Schwartz, 102–23. London: Routledge, 2015.

Scott-Clayton, Judith, Peter Crosta, and Clive Belfield. "Improving the Targeting of Treatment: Evidence from College Remediation." *Educational Evaluation and Policy Analysis* 36, no. 3 (2014): 371–93.

Scott-Clayton, Judith, and Olga Rodriguez. "Development, Discouragement, or Diversion? New Evidence on the Effects of College Remediation." *Education Finance and Policy* 10, no. 1 (2015): 4–45.

Seirawan, Hazem, Sharon Faust, and Roseann Mulligan. "The Impact of Oral Health on the Academic Performance of Disadvantaged Children." *American Journal of Public Health* 102, no. 9 (2012): 1729–34.

Shapiro, Douglas, Afet Dundar, Jin Chen, Mary Ziskin, Eunkyoung Park, Vasti Torres, and Yi-Chen Chiang. *Completing College: A National View of Student Attainment Rates.* Signature Report, National Student Clearinghouse Research Center, 2012.

Shapiro, Douglas, Afet Dundar, Fay Huie, Phoebe Wakhungu, and Ayesha Bhimdiwali. *Completing College: Eight-Year Completion Outcomes for the Fall 2010 Cohort*, Signature Report No. 12. National Student Clearinghouse Research Center, February 2019. https://nscresearchcenter.org/signaturereport12-supplement/.

Shapiro, Douglas, Afet Dundar, Fay Huie, Phoebe Wakhungu, Xin Yuan, Angel Nathan, and Ayesha Bhimdiwali. *Completing College: A National View of Student Completion Rates—Fall 2011 Cohort.* Signature Report No. 14. National Student Clearinghouse Research Center, 2017.

Shapiro, Douglas, Mikyung Ryu, Faye Huie, Quin Liu, and Yi Zheng. *Completing College 2019 National Report.* Signature Report No. 18. National Student Clearinghouse Research Center, 2019.

Sharkey, Patrick. "The Intergenerational Transmission of Context." *American Journal of Sociology* 113 (2008): 931–69.

Sharkey, Patrick, and Jacob Faber. "Where, When, Why, and for Whom Do Residential Contexts Matter? Moving Away from the Dichotomous Understanding of Neighborhood Effects." *Annual Review of Sociology* 40 (2014): 559–79. http://www.rootcausecoalition.org/wp-content/uploads/2018/09/Where-When-Why-and-For-Whom-Do-Residential-Contexts-Matter-Moving-Away-from-the-Dichotomous-Understanding-of-Neighborhood-Effects.pdf.

Shulman, James, and William Bowen. *The Game of Life: College Sports and Educational Values.* Princeton: Princeton University Press, 2011.

Stansbury, Anna, and Lawrence H. Summers. "Declining Worker Power and American Economic Performance." *Brookings Papers on Economic Activity.* Spring 2020.

Statista. "Ratio between CEOs and Average Workers in World in 2014, by Country." Statistics Portal, 2019. https://www.statista.com/statistics/424159/pay-gap-between-ceos-and-average-workers-in-world-by-country/.

Stein, Jeff. "Senior Democrats Drafting Plan to Give Parents at Least $3,000 per Child in Biden Stimulus." *Washington Post,* January 22, 2021. https://www.washingtonpost.com/us-policy/2021/01/22/biden-childtaxcredit-stimulus/.

Stiglitz, Joseph. *The Price of Inequality.* New York: W. W. Norton, 2012.

Taylor, Tim. "What Is a Gini Coefficient?" *Conversable Economist,* April 3, 2014. https://conversableeconomist.blogspot.com/2014/04/whats-gini-coefficient.html.

Tennessee Promise. tnpromise.gov.

Texas Education Agency. "Early College High School: Blueprint Redesign." 2019. https://tea.texas.gov/academics/college-career-and-military-prep/early-college-high-school.

Thernstrom, Abigail, and Stephan Thernstrom. *No Excuses: Closing the Racial Gap in Learning.* New York: Simon and Schuster, 2004.

Thompson, Sharon, Joel Myers, and T. Chris Oshima. "Student Mobility and Its Implications for Schools' Adequate Yearly Progress." *Journal of Negro Education* 80, no. 1 (2011): 12–21.

Turner, Margery, and G. Thomas Kingsley. *Federal Programs for Addressing Low-Income Housing Needs: A Policy Primer.* Washington, DC: Urban Institute, 2008.

https://www.urban.org/research/publication/federal-programs-addressing-low-income-housing-needs.

University of Wisconsin School of Education. Discussion Project. 2020. https://discussion.education.wisc.edu/.

Urban Institute. "Building a State Financial Aid Program: What Are the Trade-Offs of Different Design Choices?" 2020. https://apps.urban.org/features/how-to-build-a-state-financial-aid-program/.

———. "Nine Charts about Wealth Inequality in America." 2017. https://apps.urban.org/features/wealth-inequality-charts.

U.S. Census Bureau. American Community Survey, American Fact Finder. 2018.

———. Current Population Survey. Annual Social and Economic Supplement. 2020.

———. Current Population Survey Tables for Family Income, 2020.

———. Current Population Survey Tables for Personal Income, 2020.

———. Educational Attainment in the United States, 2020.

———. Historical Income Tables, 2020.

———. Income and Poverty in the United States, 2019.

U.S. Department of Education. Beginning Postsecondary Students Longitudinal Study, 2012/17. Institute of Education Sciences, National Center for Education Statistics, 2018. Power Stats.

———. Digest of Education Statistics, 2017. Institute of Education Sciences, National Center for Education Statistics, 2017.

———. Digest of Education Statistics, 2018. Institute of Education Sciences, National Center for Education Statistics, 2018.

———. Digest of Education Statistics, 2019. Institute of Education Sciences, National Center for Education Statistics, 2019.

———. Education Longitudinal Study of 2002. Institute of Education Sciences, National Center for Education Statistics, 2014. Power Stats.

———. "Federal Student Loan Portfolio." Federal Student Aid. 2020. https://studentaid.gov/data-center/student/portfolio/.

———. Integrated Postsecondary Education Data System. Institute of Education Sciences, National Center for Education Statistics, 2019.

———. National Postsecondary Student Aid Study, 2016. Institute of Education Sciences, National Center for Education Statistics, 2016. Power Stats.

U.S. Department of Labor. "Union Members Summary." Bureau of Labor Statistics, 2019. https://www.bls.gov/news.release/union2.nr0.htm.

Von Hippel, Paul. "Is Summer Learning Loss Real?" Education Next 19, no. 4 (Fall 2019). https://www.educationnext.org/is-summer-learning-loss-real-how-i-lost-faith-education-research-results/.

Waddell, Kaveh. "Virtual Classrooms Can Be as Unequal as Real Ones." Atlantic, September 26, 2016.

Whitford, Emma. "UVA Unveils Affordable Housing Project." *Inside Higher Ed*, March 11, 2020.

Winship, Scott. *Economic Mobility in America: A State-of-the-Art Primer.* Archbridge Institute. March 2017.

Witteveen, Dirk, and Paul Attewell. "The Earnings Payoff from Attending a Selective College." *Social Science Research* 66 (2017). https://www.researchgate.net /publication/313126425_The_earnings_payoff_from_attending_a_selective _college.

Wodtke, Geoffrey, David Harding, and Felix Elwert. "Neighborhood Effects in Temporal Perspective: The Impact of Long-Term Exposure to Concentrated Disadvantage on High School Graduation." *American Sociological Review* 76, no. 5 (2011): 713–36.

Young, Michael. *The Rise of the Meritocracy.* Abingdon: Routledge, 1958/2017.

Zucman, Gabriel. "Global Wealth Inequality." National Bureau of Economic Research Working Paper 25462. 2019.

INDEX

Page references in italics indicate a figure or table.

mobility and, 25; policy and, 144, 152, 187, 191, 197–98, 202, 209; post-college circumstances and, 113, 116, 120, 132–37, 141–42; pre-college circumstances and, 80, 106; progressive, 5–6, 14, 18, 20, 113, 120, 133, 141; reform and, 8, 136, 144; transfer system and, 8, 14–15, 25, 80, 113, 132–37, 141, 209, 211–12; transfer systems and, 8

teachers, 14, 67, 103, *104*

technology: computers, 32, 80, 166, 178–79, 206; cost-cutting by, 168, 175–81; economy and, 19, 32, 139, 199; elite institutions and, 178–80; Goldin/Katz on, 114–15; MOOCs and, 176–79; online learning and, 175–80; as savior, 175–80; skills and, 78, 114–15, 166, 199; STEM subjects and, 166; Zoom, 175, 180

test scores: ACT, 58, *64*, 67, 125, 148; post-college circumstances and, 123, 135; pre-college circumstances and, 84, 92, 95–100, 103; SAT, 58, 62–63, *64*–67, 125, 148, 193; stratification and, *63*, *64*, 68, 70

Title IV, 197

Top Ten Percent rule, 149

tuition: financial aid and, 78 (*see also* financial aid); free, 18, 142, 169–70, 174–75, 181–90, 213, 216; policy and, 147, 172, 182–95, 208; post-college circumstances and, 124, 142; pre-college circumstances and, 78, 104; selective institutions and, 69, 124, 215; spiraling costs of, 10, 183–85, 213; stratification and, 69

tutoring, 80, 154

undermatching, 73–74, 126

unemployment, 24, 90, 108, 120, 138, 141

University of Buffalo, 154
University of California-Irvine, 180
University of Texas-Austin, 149
University of Virginia, 154
University of Wisconsin-Eau Claire, 154
U.S. Department of Education, 55–56, 92
U.S. Department of Housing and Urban Development, 92
U.S. Federal Reserve Bank of New York, 71
U.S. Supreme Court, 32

violence, 103, *104*
vouchers, 91–92, 107

wages: Baby Boomers and, 15, 39; Black people and, 6, 121; college choice and, 120–25; college earnings premium and, 5, 15, 114–16, 126; disposable income and, 132–37, 142; gap in, 5, 17, 20, 115, 212; income distribution and, 2 (*see also* income distribution); international comparisons on, 127–36; lower, 14, 17–18, 115–16, 118, 120, 121n8, 138, 140–41, 212 (*see also* low-income families); market income and, 132–37, 212; median income and, 26, 44, 134, 183–84; minimum, 17–18, 115–16, 118, 120, 138, 141, 212; mobility and, 35; policy and, 182, 206; post-college circumstances and, 115–20, 121n8, 126, 137–41; pre-college circumstances and, 218; stagnation of, 116

wealth: college earnings premium and, 5, 15, 114–16, 126; disposable income and, 132–37, 142; distribution of, 3–4, 26, 28; gaps in, 1, 4, 26, 28, 123, 189; income distribution and, 3–4, 26,

wealth (*continued*)
    28, 113–14; labor market and, 8, 15,
    211; mobility and, 35–40; parental,
    1–2, 4, 39, 123, 147; policy and, 144,
    147, 151–52, 161, 182, 189, 210–11, 214–15;
    post-college circumstances and,
    123–25; pre-college circumstances
    and, 104, 106; protection from risk
    by, 24
welfare, 30–31, 137n21, 144, 210
White people: attainment and, 47–52,
    57, 58; degrees and, 14, 27, 43, 47, 48,
    58, 59, 61, 65, 122, 160; enrollment
    rates of, 52, 61, 97; great compression

and, 6; income distribution and,
26–28; mobility and, 36; policy and,
156, 160, 163; post-college circumstances and, 121, *122*; pre-college
circumstances and, 76, 78, 84, 86,
89–91, 94, 96–102, 108; selective institutions and, 62–63, *66*, 68, 217;
stratification and, *59–60*, 61–68
Whither Opportunity (research
compendium), 77

Yale University, 154

Zoom, 175, 180

CPSIA information can be obtained
at www.ICGtesting.com
Printed in the USA
LVHW111043020422
715128LV00005B/5/J

9 780691 171807